NAO National Audit Office

rse: The retention higher education

LONDON: The Stationery Office
£13.50

Ordered by the
House of Commons
to be printed on 24 July 2007

REPORT BY THE COMPTROLLER AND AUDITOR GENERAL | HC 616 Session 2006-2007 | 26 July 2007

This report has been prepared under Section 6 of the National Audit Act 1983 for presentation to the House of Commons in accordance with Section 9 of the Act.

John Bourn
Comptroller and Auditor General
National Audit Office

23 July 2007

The National Audit Office study team consisted of:

Angela Hands, Jonathan Mackay, Nick Ormiston-Smith, Sarah Perryman, Paul Wright-Anderson with the assistance of Peter Jones, Ruth Lewis, Angie MacArthur, Caroline Milligan, Nisha Patel, Tom Sawyer and Baljinder Virk.

This report can be found on the National Audit Office web site at www.nao.org.uk

For further information about the National Audit Office please contact:

National Audit Office
Press Office
157-197 Buckingham Palace Road
Victoria
London
SW1W 9SP

Tel: 020 7798 7400

Email: enquiries@nao.gsi.gov.uk

CONTENTS

Figures given in this report relate to United Kingdom domiciled undergraduates attending English institutions starting in 2004-05, unless otherwise stated.

Photographs kindly supplied by: Cover – Keith Pattison/Newcastle University; Contents, Part One – University of Liverpool; Key Facts – University of Bath; Summary and Part Two – University of Teesside; Part Three – Edge Hill University.

KEY FACTS

What constitutes higher education in England?

- Higher education courses are programmes leading to qualifications, or credits which can be counted towards qualifications, which are above the standard of A levels or equivalent qualifications. They include foundation degrees, honours degrees, undergraduate credits, higher national diplomas, higher national certificates and other higher education diplomas. (Postgraduate courses are outside the scope of this study).
- In 2005-06, there were 1.3 million undergraduates, including around 870,000 studying full time.
- 132 higher education institutions (universities and higher education colleges) and 143 further education colleges were directly funded by the Higher Education Funding Council for England (the Funding Council) for the provision of higher education in 2006-07.[1] The institutions range in size from 85 to 155,000 undergraduates (the Open University). Further education colleges have up to 3,000 higher education students (in addition to their further education learners). Higher education institutions and further education colleges are autonomous bodies.
- Most undergraduates apply for full-time courses through UCAS (formerly known as the Universities and Colleges Admissions Service), while applications for part-time courses are made directly to institutions. Institutions provide course information and hold open days for potential students and their families.

Who leads on higher education sector policy?

- The Department for Innovation, Universities and Skills (the Department) provides policy direction and funding to the Funding Council.
- The Funding Council promotes and funds teaching and some research so that the sector meets the diverse needs of students, the economy and society. The Funding Council's running costs for 2006-07 were £18 million. In the 2006-07 academic year, the Funding Council granted £6.7 billion, including £4.2 billion for teaching, to support higher education institutions and further education colleges, which represents the higher education sector's biggest source of income (as it did in 2005-06). Institutions have a range of other sources of income **(Figure 1)**, and individual institutions vary substantially in the proportion of their income that comes from each source. For example, some receive very little funding for research work, and some have much higher endowment and investment income than others.
- Academic costs are the largest component of institutions' spending **(Figure 2)**.

1 Sources of income of English institutions in 2005-06

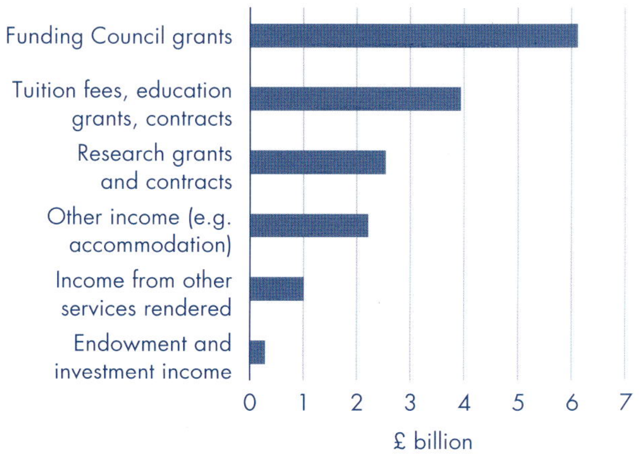

Source: Higher Education Statistics Agency (2006), Resources of Higher Education Institutions 2005-06, 'Table 1 - Income of UK HE institutions by source and location of institution 2005-06'.

1 In addition, many other further education colleges are involved in partnerships which offer higher education that the Funding Council funds through a lead higher education institution, while many also receive funding from the Learning and Skills Council for some professional and/or short higher education courses.

Why does student retention matter?

- Higher education benefits students, employers, the economy and society. Graduates earn higher salaries and contribute more, on average, to economic growth.
- Students who do not complete their studies may still gain some benefit from their experience.

How is student retention measured?

- Two main measures of retention are used throughout this report. The first is the 'completion rate' – the proportion of starters in a year who continue their studies until they obtain their qualification, with no more than one consecutive year out of higher education. As higher education courses take years to complete, an expected completion rate is calculated by the Higher Education Statistics Agency. Data to check whether the expected rates are close to the actual completion rates has only recently become available.
- A more immediate measure of retention is the proportion of an institution's intake which is enrolled in higher education in the year following their first entry to higher education. This is the 'continuation rate'.
- There are particular difficulties with data about part-time students due to the inherent flexibilities in the patterns of study, which we refer to at appropriate points in the report.

Do most students complete their courses?

- From the published performance indicators, of the 256,000 full-time, first-degree students starting higher education in 2004-05, 91.6 per cent continued into their second year. Also, the projected outcomes table shows that 78.1 per cent are expected to qualify with a first degree, with a further 2.2 per cent expected to obtain a lower qualification, and 5.8 per cent expected to transfer to another institution to continue their studies.
- From our analysis of the 50,000 part-time first-degree students starting in 2004-05, 76.9 per cent continued into their second year. Their expected completion rate is not calculated because of the lack of a consistent course structure for part-time students.
- Retention of full-time, first-degree students has improved slightly since 1999-2000 (**Figure 3**).

How does performance in England compare with other countries?

- Retention rates at English institutions in 2004-05 compare favourably with institutions in the other home nations.
- The United Kingdom compares favourably with most other countries in the Organisation for Economic Co-operation and Development, with the fifth highest estimated graduation, or 'survival', rates in 2004, behind Japan, Ireland, Korea and Greece.

2 Types of expenditure of English institutions, 2005-06

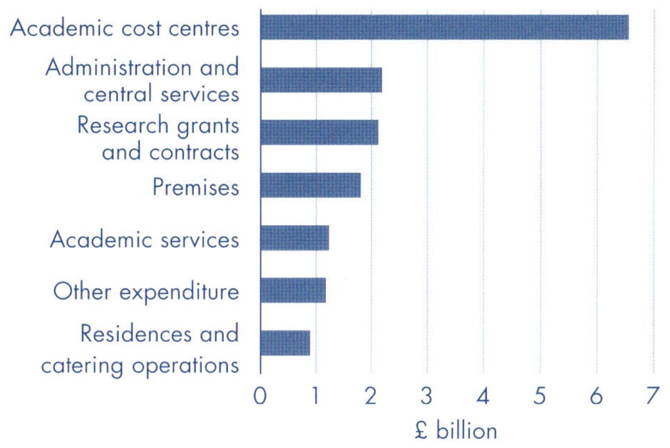

Source: Higher Education Statistics Agency (2006), Resources of Higher Education Institutions 2005-06, 'Table 2a - Expenditure of each institution by activity 2005-06'.

3 Retention of full-time, first-degree students (per cent)

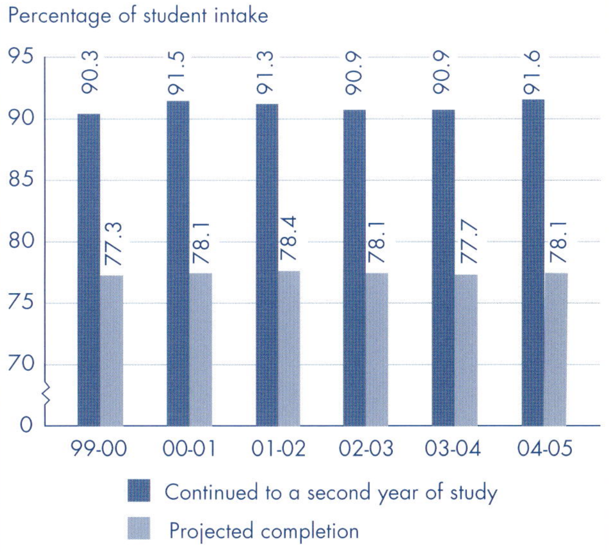

Source: National Audit Office analysis of Higher Education Statistics Agency student data

SUMMARY

1 Success in higher education will provide most students with greater opportunities for the rest of their life – over their working life graduates earn, on average, over £100,000 more (in today's terms) than similar non-graduates with A levels.[2] Employers, the economy and society as a whole also benefit when students complete their studies. The Exchequer receives associated tax from higher salaries of graduates, amounting to 11 per cent over and above the cost of higher education.

2 Around 28,000 full-time and 87,000 part-time undergraduates who commenced their studies in 2004-05 were no longer in higher education in 2005-06.[3] Substantially less value is gained from institutions' investment in teaching undergraduates who do not complete their courses.[4] The National Audit Office and the Committee of Public Accounts previously reported on the retention of students in higher education in 2002.[5] In our current examination, we considered whether the sector is improving its already high level of

2 Department for Innovation, Universities and Skills, unpublished analysis; PricewaterhouseCoopers/Universities UK (2007), The economic benefits of a degree.

3 National Audit Office calculation based on Higher Education Statistics Agency's individual student data for all undergraduates. By extrapolation, this level of non-continuation each year could represent a total cost of around £30 million in lost income over a lifetime, but this is only a rough estimate because of the uncertainty involved.

4 For example, the basic rate of Funding Council grant ranged from £2,521 to £13,684 per full-time undergraduate in 2006-07 (depending on course category), although this is not necessarily the same as the investment made by the institutions.

5 National Audit Office, Improving student achievement in English higher education, HC 486, Session 2001-02, January 2002; Committee of Public Accounts, 58th Report of 2001-02, Improving student achievement and widening participation in Higher Education in England, September 2002.

Summary text continued

performance in retaining undergraduates on their higher education courses (foundation degrees, honours degrees, undergraduate credits, higher national diplomas, higher national certificates and other higher education diplomas), focusing in particular on whether:

- the sector's performance on retention has improved since it was last reviewed by the Committee of Public Accounts (Part 1);
- the Higher Education Funding Council for England (the Funding Council) could do more to encourage the sector to improve retention of students (Part 2); and
- higher education institutions could do more to improve retention of students (Part 3).

As numbers grow, are more students completing their course?

3 The numbers of accepted applicants to higher education in the United Kingdom have increased in recent years: United Kingdom students entering via UCAS[6] increased from 332,000 in 2002-03 to 346,000 in 2006-07.[7] Applications for courses dipped in 2006, but have recovered in 2007. Between 2002 and 2006, there have been small changes in the types of subjects studied. The largest numerical increases in accepted applications have been in subjects allied to medicine and the creative arts, while the largest reductions were in mathematical and computer science, and engineering (Appendix 2, Figure 33 on page 44).

4 The sector has been seeking to both increase and widen participation to include more students from groups that have been less well represented in higher education, while bearing down on non-completion.[8] There is a balance to be achieved between these priorities, as increasing and widening participation brings in more students from under-represented groups who may need more support to complete their courses. Between the academic years 1999-2000 and 2005-06, participation in higher education increased from 39 per cent to 43 per cent of people aged between 18 and 30 years. There have also been increases in the proportions of students from a black and minority ethnic group, students with a disability, and students from a background without a tradition of higher education (Appendix 2, Figure 30 on page 43).

5 **Figure 4 overleaf** illustrates the improvement in the rate of new undergraduates in 2004-05 expected to complete their course, compared with undergraduates who started in 1999-2000. While the rate of improvement is small, it needs to be placed in the context of the United Kingdom's higher estimated graduation rate than most other countries in the Organisation for Economic Co-operation and Development (Figure 10 on page 17) and the growth in participation in higher education over the same period. It is too early to say whether the introduction of higher tuition fees from 2006-07 (up to £3,000 a year) will affect retention.

6 There are variations between subjects in the percentages of 'continuations' – first-year students who continue into the second year of their course. Medicine and Dentistry courses have by far the highest continuation rates (98 per cent) and Combined Subject courses have the lowest (83 per cent) (Figure 15 on page 21).[9] Similarly there are variations in average continuation rates between the different types of higher education institution, with The Russell Group universities[10] having the highest average continuation rate and the universities created since 1992 having the lowest average rate overall (Figure 13 on page 19).

6 UCAS was formerly known as the Universities and Colleges Admissions Service.
7 In addition, part-time students apply to institutions directly, rather than through UCAS.
8 The target is: by 2010, to increase participation in higher education towards 50 per cent of those aged 18-30 and also make significant progress year on year towards fair access and bear down on rates of non-completion.
9 Based on the National Audit Office analysis of Higher Education Statistics Agency student data for all full-time undergraduate students starting their degree in 2004-05.
10 The Russell Group is an association of 20 major research-intensive universities of the United Kingdom, including the Universities of Cambridge and Oxford. Details of the different categories of institution are set out in Section 4 of Appendix 4 on page 50.

7 Our statistical analysis indicates that variations between subjects and types of institution are largely due to the characteristics of students, including their level of pre-entry qualifications. However, when all other factors are taken into consideration, the analysis appears to show that:

- a full-time, first-degree student is much more likely to continue their studies into a second year than a similar part-time student (with an 'odds ratio' of 3.3 – see explanation of odds ratios in Note 2 to Figure 16 on page 22);
- a full-time student with three A levels at grade A is much more likely to continue than a similar student with two A levels at grade D (odds ratio of 2.2); and
- a part-time student registered with a higher education institution but taught in a further education college is more likely to continue than a similar student in a higher education institution (odds ratio of 1.6).

Could the Funding Council do more to improve retention?

8 The Department for Innovation, Universities and Skills has overall responsibility for public spending on higher education in England and, pursuant to its objective of raising and widening participation, has set a key target to bear down on rates of non-completion. The Funding Council has been delegated responsibilities to account for the proper use of public money, and to provide assurance that the higher education sector is managed effectively and that value for money is being achieved. For the 2006-07 academic year, the Funding Council allocated £6.7 billion to the sector.

9 In its oversight of the sector, the Funding Council recognises institutions' autonomy. Regulatory activity to maintain accountability for public funds is determined by design of the funding method and by whether institutions comply with the conditions the Funding Council attaches to their grant. The Funding Council also works as an enabler in partnership with institutions and other organisations. It aims to improve retention by incentivising and penalising institutions through its funding arrangements and by promoting improvements by publication of performance information, and by facilitating the sharing of good practice.

4 Progress on increasing participation and retention

The sector has made progress on increasing participation and, to a lesser extent, expected completion rates since 1999-2000.

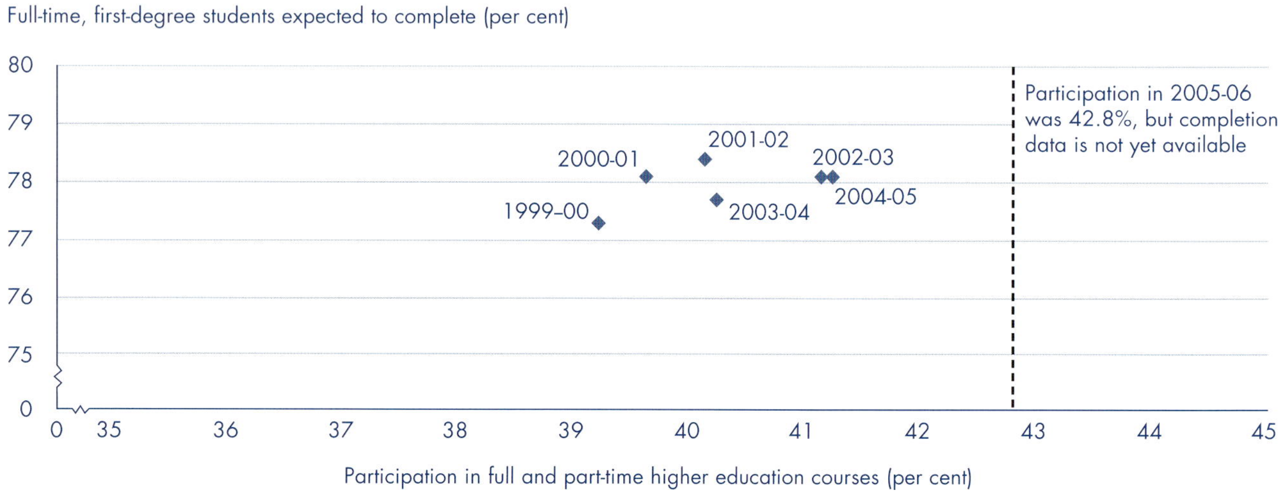

Source: National Audit Office analysis of Higher Education Statistics Agency indicators and the then Department for Education and Skill's Statistical First Release 140/2007

NOTE

Participation is measured by the Higher Education Initial Participation Rate statistic which calculates the proportion of English 17-30 year olds participating in higher education in the United Kingdom for the first time.

10 One of the Funding Council's key performance targets is to maintain or improve the proportion of full-time, first-degree students in English higher education institutions who continue into their second year. The target includes only these students because of the lack of a suitable dataset for the other students: for example, the Funding Council considers that retention data is difficult to interpret due to a lack of inconsistent course structure.

11 In 2002, the Committee of Public Accounts recommended that the Funding Council should continue to bear down on wide variations in performance between institutions, focusing on underperforming institutions. Although institutions' continuation rates fell within a slightly narrower range in 2004-05 **(Figure 5)** compared with 2001-02, our tests showed no statistically significant difference in the distribution.[11] We examined how the continuation rate of each institution had changed between 2001-02 and 2004-05. Of the 117 institutions with data available for both years, 42 (36 per cent) increased their continuation rate by at least one percentage point. The continuation rate of 30 institutions (26 per cent) decreased by at least one percentage point and 45 institutions (38 per cent) remained about the same. If all of the institutions had achieved at least the same rate as in 2001-02, then an additional 1,250 students would have continued into a second year of study and the national continuation rate for 2004-05 would have been 92.1 per cent rather than 91.6 per cent.

12 To inform a more meaningful assessment of performance, the Higher Education Statistics Agency[12] calculates a benchmark for each institution, which takes account of students' entry qualifications and subjects studied.[13] Because the benchmark is an average based on students in all institutions in the United Kingdom, some institutions will be above the benchmark and some below. A small number of institutions with apparently low continuation rates but with larger than average numbers of students with, for example, relatively low entry qualifications, outperform their benchmark. For most institutions in 2004-05, actual continuation and benchmark figures were similar: 73 per cent of institutions in the top quarter for continuation rates remained in the top half after adjustment for their benchmark, while 13 per cent of institutions in the bottom quarter moved to the top half after adjustment. Nineteen per cent of institutions were at least two percentage points below their benchmark.[14]

5 Continuation rates in all institutions, 2004-05

Continuation rates at most institutions are between 85 per cent and 96 per cent.

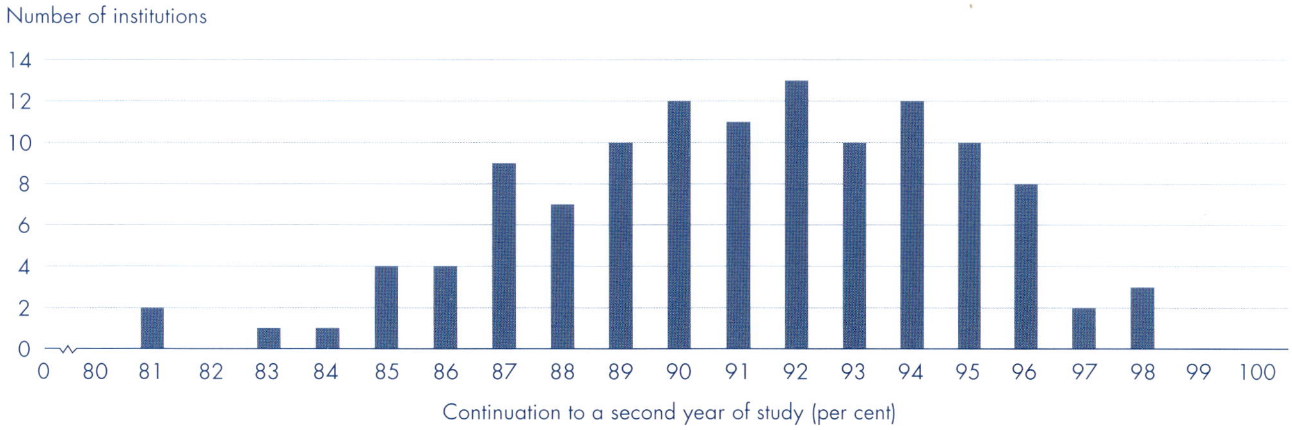

Source: National Audit Office analysis of Higher Education Statistics Agency student data

NOTE

This analysis is based on full-time, first-degree students.

11 Based on Levene's Equality of Variance test, which is a reliable statistical test that compares variances in different sample groups.

12 The Higher Education Statistics Agency is the official agency for the collection, analysis and dissemination of data about higher education. It is a company limited by guarantee and its members are the two representative bodies for higher education institutions in the United Kingdom – Universities UK and GuildHE.

13 The Higher Education Statistics Agency does this on behalf of the Performance Indicators Steering Group, which represents the sector, including the Department and the Funding Council, and is responsible for overseeing the development of performance indicators.

14 It is to be expected that some institutions are below their benchmark and others above, because the benchmark is an average based on students in all institutions in the United Kingdom.

13 Institutions have considerable flexibility in how they distribute their funding internally. And as the Funding Council is concerned with outcomes rather than inputs, it does not 'ring fence' the majority of its funding (the teaching grant) but allocates it as a block grant based on the numbers of students completing a year of study, the subject mix and other institutional and student-related cost factors. If the actual numbers vary widely from those on which the grant is based, then the Funding Council will hold back part of an institution's grant in-year and reduce it in the following year. However, institutions can recover the following year's reduction if they make good their position in the subsequent year.

14 Since 1999-2000, the Funding Council has allocated a small proportion of its teaching grant based on the types of students recruited, recognising that students from under-represented groups or with lower entry qualifications are likely to cost more to teach and retain, and counteracting a disincentive to recruit them. Most of this funding (£345 million in 2006-07) was reallocated from existing funding so it did not represent additional investment. In particular there was a large increase in widening participation funding in 2003-04 with the establishment of a new stream for improving retention, which was financed by a reduction in the rest of the teaching grant. This has resulted in some institutions gaining funding and others losing funding. Our analysis did not find conclusive evidence regarding the impact on institutions' continuation rates from this change in funding in 2003-04, owing to there being only a small number of years of data available.

15 The Higher Education Statistics Agency publishes a range of performance information on institutions, including the Higher Education Performance Indicators, listing institutions' retention of students. In addition, the results of the National Student Survey are available, along with other information, on the Teaching Quality Information website. As well as helping make institutions accountable, publication of the performance information provides an external incentive for institutions to improve retention because it affects their reputation and hence their student recruitment.

16 The Funding Council and some of its partners also have a role in encouraging the sharing of good practice on retention and related issues, which they aim to fulfil primarily through additional funding of certain institutions to share good practice. The sector has access to a wide range of advice on good practice in retention, although we found that there is relatively little evaluation of the impact and transferability of practice.

Could institutions do more to improve retention?

17 Students leave their courses early for a range of reasons, but there is rarely one single reason why a student gives up their course (Appendix 3). Reasons are likely to be a mix of personal (most common), institution and course related, and financial (case examples in Figure 17 on page 23).

18 Much of what an institution does is likely to affect the quality of the student experience and therefore student success and retention. However there are a number of specific activities that institutions are using to enhance retention, and important activities are set out in **Figure 6**. There are two especially important areas where we concluded that an institution can target their work and make a difference. These are:

- getting to really know their students and how, generally, they feel about their particular course of study and the culture and amenities offered in the institution; and
- developing a more positive approach to retention-related activities that recognises how they can also improve student success, and so attract students to take up services who might otherwise not do so.

These activities can involve extra costs that institutions may defray using the funding redistributed by the Funding Council (paragraph 14).

6 Actions to improve retention

Action	Description
Management information	Most institutions collate and disseminate internal information on withdrawal rates at course and faculty level. Others also use student level information, for example on attendance, to identify students at risk of withdrawal. A minority of institutions conduct periodic exercises to contact early leavers to help establish the real reasons why they left, particularly where some common issue affecting retention is indicated.
Strategic commitment to retention	It is important for institutions to have a clear strategic commitment to retaining students that all staff understand and buy into, so that they can see how commitment to high levels of retention should affect the way they work. All the institutions we visited were undertaking some activities to improve retention, but not all were based on a clear strategy for the whole organisation. Even at institutions where the strategy was clear, senior managers acknowledged that some parts of their institution were demonstrating greater commitment than others.
Commitment from students	Students need to commit to attending lectures and carrying out independent study. Universities can communicate this clearly to students and follow up cases where commitment seems not to have been secured.
Support through academic provision	Properly resourced tutoring systems help individual students to identify the extra support and facilities they can use to improve their chances of success. Institutions often offer pre-entry courses and learning support opportunities, but many institutions find it difficult to get students to take up services that would help them to 'stay the course' and succeed. This can be because students and academic staff may regard the services as being there to fill a 'deficit' in a student's ability, but institutions can increase take-up by promoting these services as positive options to take to improve the prospects of a good degree.
Broaden options for learning	Some institutions, and in particular those with higher numbers of non-traditional students, are being flexible in allowing students to choose learning options to fit their personal circumstances, for example through comprehensive modular systems.
Provide specialist support	All institutions provide specialist support services, such as welfare. They are increasingly organised as a 'one stop shop', and student unions usually have an important role in their provision. Financial support, through bursaries and hardship funds, is available to assist students from disadvantaged backgrounds or in financial difficulty. Some institutions are more proactive in promoting financial support than others.

Source: National Audit Office case study visits and literature review

19 We identified a common issue across institutions relating to students with disabilities. Some students with disabilities are entitled to financial assistance (Disabled Students' Allowances), with the funding coming from the Department. We found that students receiving an Allowance are much more likely to continue their course than other students self-declaring a disability and, indeed, than students who are not disabled.[15] Although the number receiving an Allowance has increased, at some institutions an Allowance is obtained by less than 10 per cent of self-declared disabled students studying full time or at least more than half time, and at other institutions over 70 per cent obtain an Allowance. Organisations that provide institutions with support and advice in respect of students with disabilities include the Equality Challenge Unit and the Disability Rights Commission.

Overall conclusions and recommendations

20 Compared internationally, higher education in England achieves high levels of student retention. For the sector to improve even marginally on that level of performance while, at the same time, opening up higher education to both increased numbers and greater diversity of students is a big challenge. The improvements so far are a good achievement.

21 The gap between higher education institutions with the highest and lowest levels of retention (taking account of their student and subject profiles), and a minority of institutions' worsening continuation rates indicate, however, that there is scope for some further improvements in retention. The types of actions that institutions can take to improve retention need not be expensive and usually also improve the student experience and contribute to a better quality education, leading to better value for money for students and from public funds. Furthermore, these actions will become increasingly important as moves to further increase and widen participation bring in more students who are likely to need support.

22 As autonomous bodies, most of the impetus and actions for sustaining and improving retention rest with higher education institutions. The Funding Council will (where consistent with the remit and priorities in its annual grant letter from the Secretary of State for Innovation, Universities and Skills) collaborate with institutions to assist them in implementing our recommendations, outlined below. A major aim of the collaboration will be to consult with the sector on the most effective approaches to achieving improvement, and to stimulate the identification, evaluation and dissemination of good practice. We consider, and the Funding Council agrees, that it will be particularly important for the Funding Council to engage with those institutions that have suffered from declining retention in recent years. All institutions should consider the recommendations in the context of the particular retention issues that each institution faces. With the co-operation of the National Audit Office's study team, the Funding Council will draw on the information, analysis and lessons from the study in facilitating higher education institutions' responses, so that the maximum possible improvements to levels of student retention are achieved.

a Levels of student retention are an important indicator of institutional health. Building on existing performance indicators, all governing bodies should periodically review trends in retention, including across different parts of the institution and for different student groups, for example for part-time students, and for particular subjects. The frequency and depth of review should be proportionate to the seriousness of any retention issues that need to be addressed. Institutions can gain the maximum benefit from the review by also using the results to improve the student experience and develop their strategies for learning and teaching.

b Monitoring of retention should be carried out at student, faculty and course level, so that it underpins work at faculty and course level to improve student retention or sustain existing good levels of retention.

15 While the Allowances make it easier for disabled students to study, it may also be the case that successful applicants for the Allowances display greater persistence generally and so are more likely also to succeed in their studies.

c Where particular problems with student retention are indicated, early leaver surveys should be undertaken to improve institutions' understanding of why students leave and what might have been done differently to support them to stay.

d Student support, including tutoring systems that provide sufficient access to academic staff, should positively emphasise the opportunity to improve grades rather than simply addressing learning deficits. Academic and administrative staff should review systems and processes in this light.

e Institutions need to know whether their students who are likely to be eligible for Disabled Students' Allowances are obtaining it and, if not, how to provide students with better support to apply.

f Institutions can improve by adopting good practice from elsewhere in the sector, and by spreading good practice more widely within their own institution. In particular, institutions can explore differences in retention performance with other institutions that have broadly comparable recruitment, curriculum and retention benchmarks.

In addition, in the course of our study, we discussed the following three specific actions with the Funding Council, which the Council has agreed to take.

g The Funding Council will work with the sector to develop, if feasible, performance indicators with appropriate benchmarks for the retention of part-time students.

h Now that a longer time series data is available, the Funding Council will use the data to verify that the projections of expected completion rates are sufficiently close to the actual completion rates achieved by institutions.

i In the light of the National Audit Office's work, the Funding Council will commission research into how far the apparent differences between institutions in students' receipt of Disabled Students' Allowances reflect eligible students missing out on their entitlement. On this basis, it will then work with the Equality Challenge Unit and Disability Rights Commission[16] to improve institutions' support to students to apply, and advise the Department for Innovation, Universities and Skills on how the Department may contribute to reaching and assisting potential applicants.

16 The Disability Rights Commission becomes part of the new Commission for Equality and Human Rights in October 2007.

The importance of retaining students

1.1 Higher education benefits students, employers, the economy and society as a whole. The Department for Innovation, Universities and Skills estimates that over their working life graduates earn, on average, over £100,000 more (in today's terms) than similar non-graduates with A levels. The Exchequer receives the associated tax benefits which PricewaterhouseCoopers estimated will for 2006-07 entrants be equivalent to a return of 11 per cent on the costs to the state of providing higher education.[17] Public funding for teaching undergraduates is substantial, with grants to institutions ranging from £2,521 to £13,684 per student in 2006-07, in addition to further public contributions that may be made towards students' tuition fees.[18]

1.2 Our interviews with 17 former students and wider research demonstrate that students who do not complete their course may still gain skills, confidence and important life experience from higher education. However, they sometimes fear stigma and omit their experience from their curriculum vitae.[19] However, withdrawal need not mean the end of an academic career – one in five full-time undergraduates who withdraw early return to study in the following year[20], and more follow later. Institutions can contribute to 'lifelong learning' – the continuance of education throughout adult life – by accepting the transfer of academic credit between courses and institutions, and allowing students to take a break in their studies.

1.3 In this part of the report we:

- examine progress towards national targets for completion, and how England compares with other countries;
- analyse the range of performance between institutions; and
- identify which students are at greatest risk of leaving early, and summarise why students leave.

A much higher proportion of full-time students complete their course than students studying part time

1.4 Higher education courses take years to complete, particularly for students studying part time and for those taking a break in their studies. **Figure 7** illustrates the outcomes for two cohorts of students. It shows that most full-time, first-degree students completed their chosen course within four years, and at that point about 15 per cent had left higher education without qualifying. Forty-seven percent of part-time, first-degree students had completed within six years, whilst at that point 44 per cent had left education without qualifying.

1.5 There are particular difficulties with data about part-time students due to the inherent flexibilities in the patterns of study and time taken to complete a course. The conclusions drawn from data on part-time students therefore need to be treated with caution. A recommendation from a review in autumn 2006 of the sector's performance indicators was that an initial study should be undertaken to look at non-continuation and completion for part-time students. An indicator would be developed from this work if appropriate. This study is being carried out by the Funding Council in conjunction with the Performance Indicators Steering Group.[21]

17 Following full implementation of top-up fees and student finance reform. PricewaterhouseCoopers/Universities UK (2007), *The economic benefits of a degree*.
18 Grants to institutions per full-time equivalent student are higher for more expensive courses such as those requiring laboratory work.
19 Quinn, J et al (2005), *From life crisis to lifelong learning: Rethinking working-class 'drop out' from higher education*, Joseph Rowntree Foundation.
20 Higher Education Statistics Agency Performance Indicators: Table T4a – Resumption of study in 2005/06, after year out of HE in 2004/05: Full-time first degree entrants 2003/04.
21 The Higher Education Statistics Agency does this on behalf of the Performance Indicators Steering Group which represents the sector.

7 Educational outcomes for full-time and part-time, first-degree students

Most full-time, first-degree students starting in 2002-03 had completed their qualification after four years. Under half of the part-time students starting in 2000-01 had completed their studies after six years.

Outcome	Full-time, first-degree students commencing 2002-03 %	Part-time, first-degree students commencing 2000-01 %
Achieved	**76.8** of which:	**46.9** of which:
First degree at original institution	70.4	37.1
First degree at a different institution	3.7	3.6
Lower level qualification	2.7	6.2
Still studying	**8.1** of which:	**8.7** of which:
For a first degree at the original institution	5.0	4.7
For a first degree at a different institution	2.6	2.4
For a lower level qualification	0.5	1.6
Left higher education without qualifying	**15.2**	**44.5**
	100.0	**100.0**

Source: Unpublished analysis carried out for this study by the Higher Education Funding Council for England

NOTE

The results in this table are indicative only for the following reasons:

- it covers two single cohorts only, and different cohorts may show different outcomes. For example, the part-time students starting now may in time achieve a different pattern of outcomes to those who started in 2000-01. The results therefore are not sufficiently robust for use as an ongoing national measure.
- The Funding Council considers that data on part-time students is difficult to interpret due to the lack of a consistent course structure.
- The analysis excludes Open University students, which in 2000-01 recorded all students as registering for modules rather than first degrees. Open University students account for approximately half of all part-time, first degree students.

1.6 Because of the years required to complete studies, it takes a long time to produce reliable statistics on course outcomes for cohorts of students. Until very recently, there was insufficient time series data for the Higher Education Statistics Agency to calculate actual completion rates, and it used instead a statistical method to estimate **expected completion**. A more immediate measure of student retention is **continuation** from the first year into the second year of study. Full-time students are more likely than part-time students to continue studying into their second year. Our analysis of the Higher Education Statistics Agency data demonstrates that of those starting courses in 2004-05:

- 90.6 per cent of full-time students continued into a second year of study (including 91.6 per cent of those studying for a first degree); and
- 61.9 per cent of part-time students continued into a second year of study (including 76.9 per cent of those studying for a first degree).

The Funding Council's target is to maintain or improve retention rates

1.7 To achieve a 100 per cent rate of completion is neither possible nor desirable in a mass higher education system. No other country achieves it and, for some students, leaving a course early is a rational response to life events, while others may have achieved their objectives or withdraw to pursue a new opportunity.

1.8 The Government has a target for higher education which reflects the need for a balance between increasing participation and improving or maintaining completion rates, and requires the higher education sector to increase and to widen participation while 'bearing down' on levels of non-completion.[22] The progress that the sector has made on these objectives in recent years is illustrated in Figure 4 (page 8) and in Appendix 2.

1.9 To support this, the Funding Council has its own target for the sector to maintain or improve the proportion of new students continuing to a second year of study, compared with 2002-03. The target includes only full-time, first-degree students at higher education institutions, because the Funding Council considers that data on part-time students is difficult to interpret due to the lack of a consistent course structure.

22 The Government's target is: by 2010, increase participation in higher education towards 50 per cent of those aged 18-30 and also make significant progress year on year towards fair access and bear down on rates of non-completion. A technical note on how the target is measured and achievement defined is at www.dfes.gov.uk/aboutus/reports/docs/SR04PSATargetsTechNotes-updated-2007-05-15.doc.

1.10 The Funding Council is working with the sector to encourage continuous improvement in both continuation into the second year and completion. The proportions of full-time, first degree students continuing to the second year and expected to complete improved for students starting in 2000-01, and were at a similar level for students starting in 2004-05 **(Figure 8)**.

1.11 Students in English institutions are more likely to continue and complete their studies than those in institutions in Scotland, Wales and Northern Ireland **(Figure 9)**.

1.12 It appears that students in the United Kingdom are more likely to complete their course of study than those in most other countries in the Organisation for Economic Co-operation and Development **(Figure 10)**. In 2004 the United Kingdom had the fifth highest 'survival' rate (an estimate of the proportion of new students who graduate), although there are some simplifications in the estimations.

8 Continuation and expected completion rates, 1996-97 to 2004-05

For full-time, first-degree students, the rate of continuation to a second year of study and expected completion rate rose in 2000-01, fell back slightly and then increased in 2004-05.

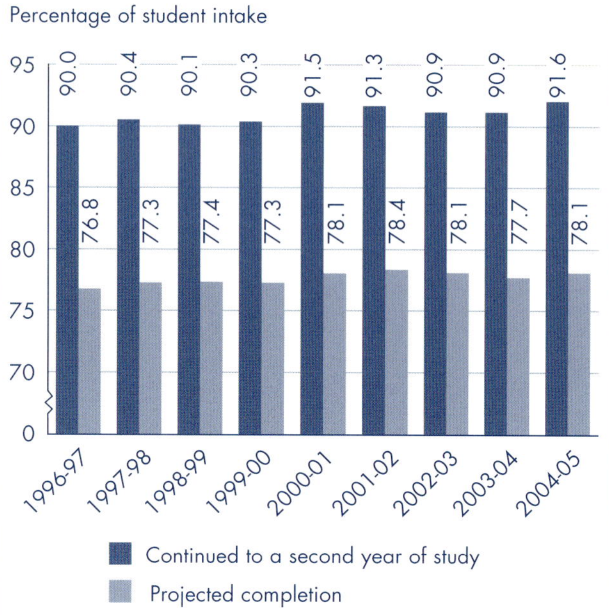

Source: Higher Education Statistics Agency's and Higher Education Funding Council for England's performance indicators

NOTE

Students who transfer to another institution are counted as 'continuers'. They are not included amongst the 'completers' because of the way that the calculations are done.

Retention rates vary between institutions

1.13 Institutions are diverse and differ in the types of students they enrol: some select those with high A level scores, while others commonly recruit students without traditional qualifications. This affects institutions' rates of retention because students with higher entry qualifications are more likely, on average, to complete their course.

1.14 In 2002, the Committee of Public Accounts concluded that there was a wide range in institutions' performance and recommended that the Funding Council should address under-performance by institutions. Institutions' continuation rates had a similar distribution in 2004-05 as in 2001-02: our tests showed no statistically significant difference in the distribution.[23] We examined how the continuation rate of each institution had changed between 2001-02 and 2004-05 **(Figure 11 overleaf)**. Of the 117 institutions with data available for both years, 42 (36 per cent) increased their continuation rate by one percentage point or more. The continuation rate of 30 institutions (26 per cent) decreased by at least one percentage point and 45 institutions (38 per cent) were within one percentage point of their level in 2001-02.

9 The retention of students starting courses by home nation, 2004-05

Students in England are more likely to continue to a second year of study and complete their courses than students in Scotland, Wales and Northern Ireland.

	Percentage of students continuing to a second year of study	Percentage of students expected to complete their course
England	91.6	78.1
Wales	89.7	77.1
Scotland	89.3	73.8
Northern Ireland	89.7	77.9
United Kingdom	**91.2**	**77.6**

Source: Higher Education Statistics Agency

NOTE

Based on full-time, first-degree students only.

23 Based on Levene's Equality of Variance test.

10 International 'survival' rates in 2004

The United Kingdom has high rates of graduation in comparison with many other countries.[1]

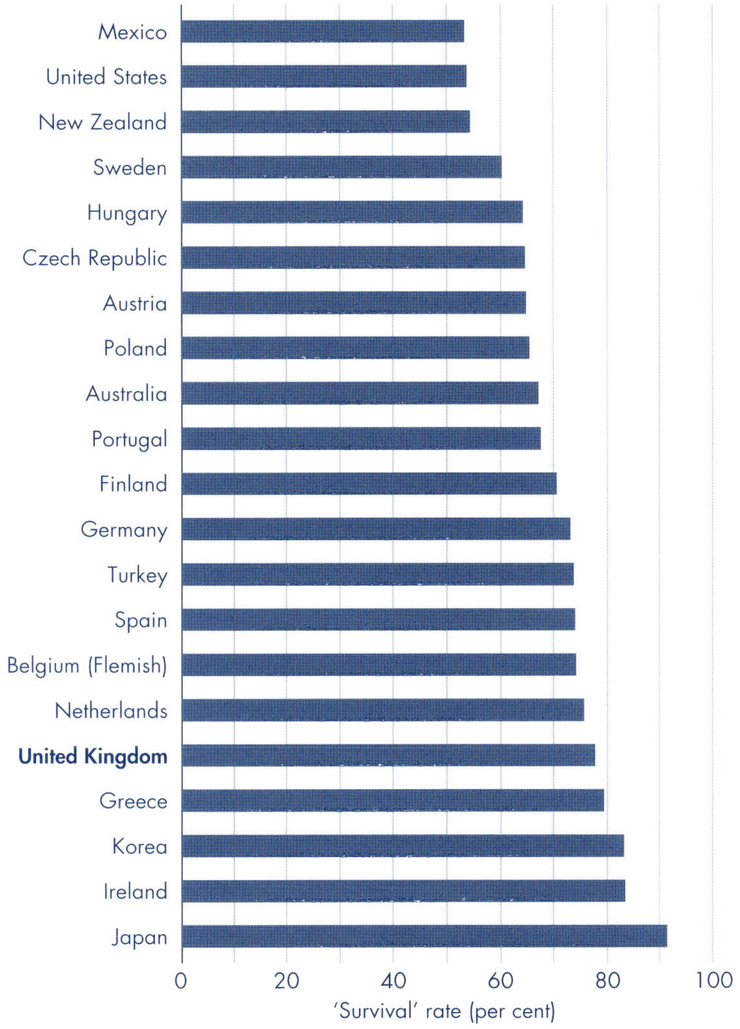

Source: Organisation for Economic Co-operation and Development (2006), Education at a Glance, 2006: 'Table A3.2. Survival rates in tertiary education'

NOTES

1 This chart shows survival rates for courses ('Tertiary-type A programmes') that are largely theory-based and provide qualifications for entry into advanced research and high-skill professions. Differences between countries' results reflect the way education systems are organised, including entry requirements and student finance, and the way that countries compile their statistics. They do not necessarily indicate that a country's higher education sector performs better or worse.

2 The estimated survival rate is the number of new graduates divided by the number of entrants admitted in previous years, with a time lag equivalent to the length of a typical full-time degree (http://stats.oecd.org/glossary/detail.asp?ID=5434). The Organisation makes some simplifications in its estimations of entrants to higher education: for example, it includes all entrants (not just new entrants) and overseas students. In countries where students often move between institutions, these students are counted as a starter each time they change, but only once on graduation, which tends to reduce the estimated survival rate. The calculation does not take into account changes in qualification aim: for example, a student who registers for a module rather than a whole degree, but then goes on to complete a degree is not included as an entrant but is included as a graduate. It is therefore important to bear in mind that the figures produced by each country are not strictly comparable.

1.15 In view of the sector's high continuation rates, there are limited ways in which increases in continuation might reasonably be expected. We examined the scope for further improvements using two measures based on: increasing continuation in institutions achieving below the national average; and recovering an earlier continuation rate in institutions whose continuation rates have reduced. Both methods below indicated that an additional 1,250 full-time, first-degree students in 2004-05 might have continued from their first year to their second year.

- Method 1 – each of the 58 institutions achieving a continuation rate below the national average increases its rate by one percentage point.
- Method 2 – each of the 51 institutions with a lower continuation rate in 2004-05 compared with 2001-02 maintains its 2001-02 continuation rate.

1.16 An additional 1,250 continuing full-time, first-degree students would have increased the national rate for continuation in 2004-05 from 91.6 per cent to 92.1 per cent. Between 2001-02 and 2004-05 the actual improvement achieved was from 91.3 per cent to 91.6 cent. Over the same period the actual numbers of students participating in higher education were also increasing.

1.17 Institutions vary widely in their success in retaining part-time students from a first into a second continuous year of study, ranging from 48 per cent to 94 per cent of students **(Figure 12)**. Part-time students are more likely to follow their courses on a flexible pathway and to have breaks in their studies which will contribute to their continuation rates being lower as a result.

1.18 The higher education sector can be divided into four main groups of institution. On average, The Russell Group universities have the highest continuation rates for full-time students and the universities created after 1992 have the lowest rates overall **(Figure 13)**. These broad variations largely reflect the types of students they enrol and their level of pre-entry qualifications.

11 Change in institutions' continuation rates from 2001-02 to 2004-05

The majority of institutions improved their continuation rates.

Source: National Audit Office analysis of Higher Education Statistics Agency student data

NOTE

Based on full-time, first-degree students only.

12 Institutions' rates of continuation to a second year of study for part-time, first-degree students, 2004-05

The proportion of part-time students who continue to a second year of study varies by institution.

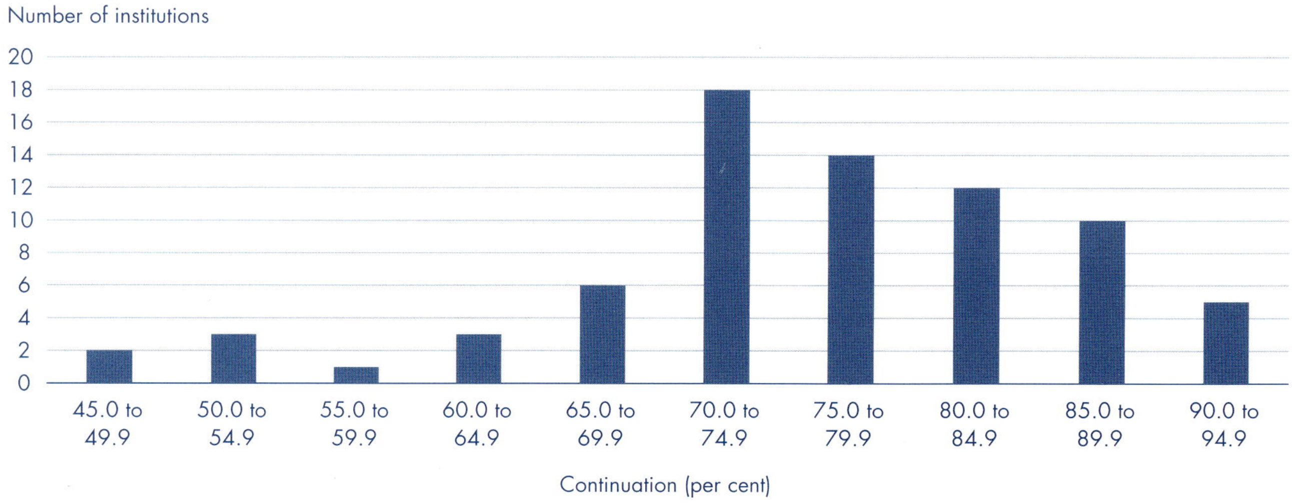

Source: National Audit Office analysis of Higher Education Statistics Agency student data

NOTE

The analysis is based on all 74 institutions with 50 or more part-time students. It includes the Open University which accounts for a large proportion of part-time students.

13 Continuation rates for full-time, first-degree students by type of institution, 2004-05

Different groups of institutions achieve varying continuation rates, with The Russell Group institutions having the highest average rates.

The Russell Group (15)

Pre-1992 universities (excluding The Russell Group) (24)

Small and specialist institutions (35)

Post-1992 universities (45)

Guide to interpreting the chart

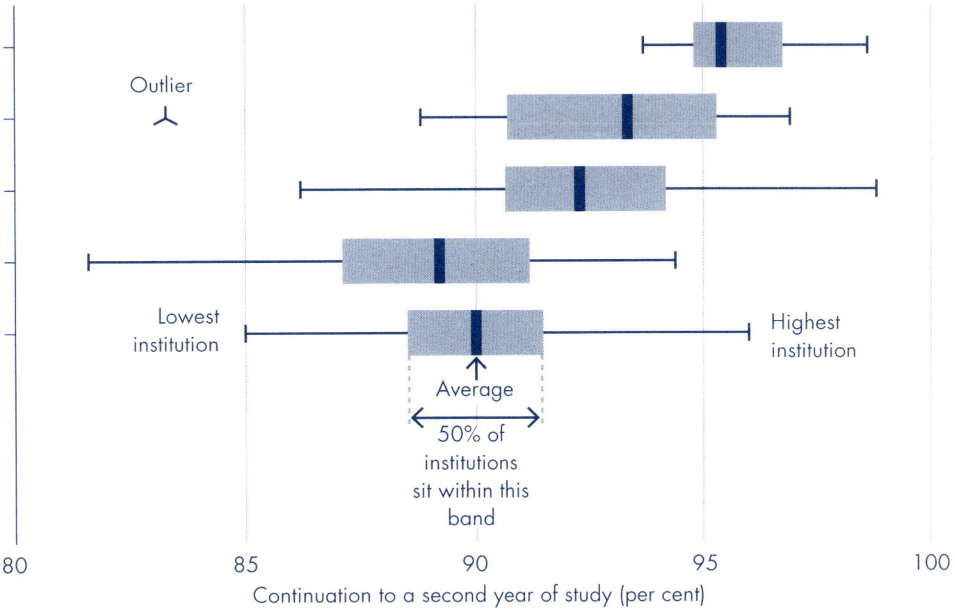

Source: National Audit Office analysis of Higher Education Statistics Agency student data

NOTES

1 Based on continuation figures for 119 English institutions providing data for full-time, first-degree students starting their courses in 2004-05. The 'outlier' is a very small institution, where each student represents three percent of the continuation rate.

2 See Appendix 4 for the classification of individual institutions.

1.19 To make meaningful comparisons between institutions, the Higher Education Statistics Agency calculates a retention benchmark for each institution. An institution's benchmark is the average continuation rate of the sector, adjusted for the entry qualifications and subjects of study of their students. A small number of institutions with apparently low absolute continuation rates achieve a level of retention above their benchmark. For example, the University of Teesside was 72nd out of 119 institutions in absolute terms in 2004-05, but was 15th when measured against its benchmark. Other institutions with apparently high absolute continuation rates perform less well compared with their benchmark (Appendix 2, Figure 28 and Figure 29). In some cases, institutions' performance can be affected by special circumstances that are not taken into account in their benchmark such as a recent merger with another institution. Institutions with the highest and lowest continuation rates in 2004-05, in headline terms and compared with their benchmark, are shown in **Figure 14 overleaf**.

1.20 Our statistical analysis indicated that four factors explain over 70 per cent of the difference between institutions in the proportion of full-time students continuing to a second year of study (Appendix 4, Section 1). Continuation is higher for institutions which:

- recruit more students from neighbourhoods with higher rates of participation in higher education;
- admit students with higher pre-entry qualifications;
- have a smaller proportion of their intake aged 21 or over; and
- offer particular subjects – in particular, institutions are more likely to have high continuation rates where they have more students studying education, Medicine and Dentistry, subjects allied to Medicine and the Creative Arts.

Some types of student are less likely to finish their course

1.21 Students on particular courses are more likely to stay the course than others. Absolute continuation rates between subjects vary, with Medicine and Dentistry having by far the highest continuation rates, and Combined subject degrees and Mathematical and Computer Sciences having the lowest rates among all undergraduates **(Figure 15)**. As with the variations between the types of institution, much of the variation reflects the types of students enrolled and their level of pre-entry qualifications.

1.22 We calculated the chances of different types of full-time and part-time students continuing into a second year, adjusting for a number of other course and student characteristics (**Figure 16 overleaf**; Appendix 4, Section 2). Students of similar types are not evenly distributed across the sector, and those less likely to continue may in part be a reflection of the practices of the institutions that tend to recruit those students as well as reflecting the characteristics of the students themselves.

1.23 The factor most affecting a student's chance of continuing is whether they are studying full time or part time, with full-time students being much more likely to continue if other factors are held constant (with an 'odds ratio' of 3.3 – see note 2 to Figure 16 on page 22). There are also substantial differences in the effect that other factors have on the continuation rates of these two groups:

- for full-time students, the biggest influence on likelihood of continuation is entry qualifications;
- part-time students, in particular, who have previously obtained a foundation degree – which then offers a student part exemption from a degree course – have an improved chance of continuing on the degree course;
- part-time students registered with a higher education institution for a course which is taught in a further education college are more likely to continue than those in higher education institutions, whereas the opposite is true among the full-time cohort; and
- both full and part-time students who declare a disability are slightly more likely to continue than those without a (declared) disability when all other factors are held constant.

1.24 In response to a request by the Secretary of State, the Funding Council convened an advisory group that identified modern foreign languages and a range of science, technology, engineering and mathematical subjects as strategically important to the nation, where provision may be vulnerable to low demand for places but intervention could support provision. In addition, courses

14 Institutions with the highest and lowest continuation rates, 2004-05

	Continuation (per cent)	Benchmark for continuation (per cent)	Difference
Institutions with highest absolute continuation rate			
St George's Hospital Medical School	98.8	95.0	3.8
University of Oxford	98.6	97.3	1.3
Institutions with highest continuation rate in comparison with benchmark			
Conservatoire for Dance and Drama	95.8	89.8	6.0
St Mary's University College (Twickenham)	94.4	89.8	4.6
Institutions with lowest absolute and relative continuation rates			
University of Bolton	81.6	86.3	–4.7
University of Chester	81.7	90.1	–8.4

Source: Higher Education Statistics Agency

NOTES

1 This analysis is based on institutions with 200 or more full-time, first-degree students only, since the continuation rates of smaller institutions are more variable, year on year.

2 The University of Chester considers that its continuation rate for 2004-05 suffered from the short-term effect of its takeover of the provision of a local further education college. Its continuation rate in 2003-04 was 4.9 percentage points below its benchmark.

requiring laboratories, studios and fieldwork tend to be more expensive to teach, and the Funding Council pays institutions a higher teaching grant per student than for classroom-based subjects.

1.25 When science, technology, engineering and mathematics students are considered together, they are less likely to continue to a second year of study than students following other subjects. There are variations between these subjects, with students taking Computer Science, Mechanical Engineering and Electronic Engineering less likely to continue. Full-time students taking modern foreign languages are also less likely to continue than students taking other subjects, after adjusting for other factors such as entry qualifications.

Students leave throughout the academic year and for a range of reasons

1.26 Contrary to the views of some commentators, our analysis suggested that the first term was not the most common time to leave: in fact, more students are recorded as having withdrawn in the summer term, around the traditional examination time, although this could reflect inaccuracies in the recording of leaving dates.[24] Three per cent of full-time, first-degree students transfer to a different institution for their second year: these students are counted as continuers.

15 Continuation rates by subject, 2004-05

Students following some subjects are more likely to continue to a second year than others.

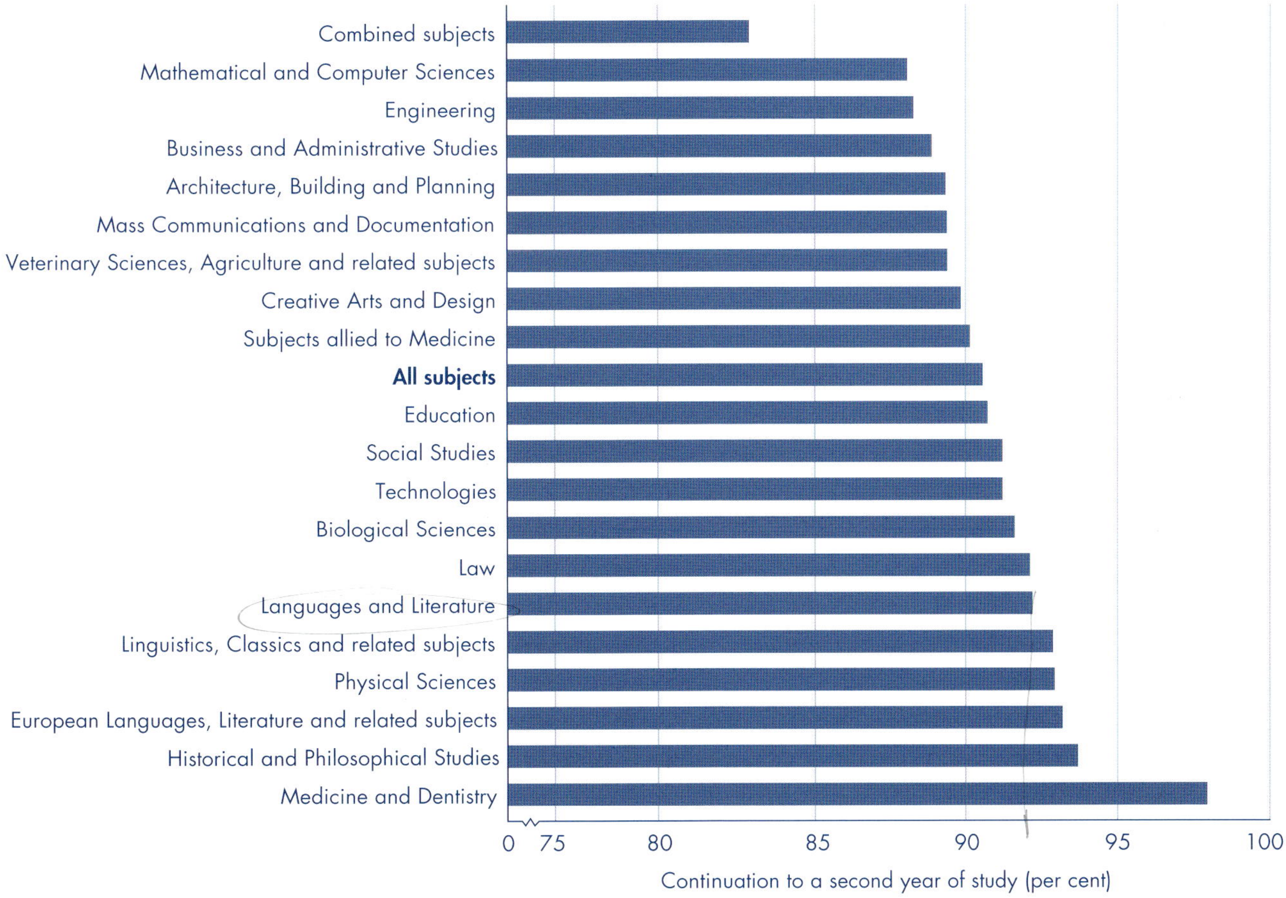

Source: National Audit Office analysis of Higher Education Statistics Agency student data

NOTE
Based on full-time, first-year undergraduate students.

24 Full-time, first-degree students may have ceased attending earlier but not be recorded as leaving until they fail or do not take their assessment.

16 Personal and study characteristics and the likelihood of continuing into a second year of study

When all other characteristics are held constant, entry qualifications are important to chances of continuing to a second year of study, as are a wide range of personal characteristics.[1]

Characteristic	The ratio of the chances of the first group of students continuing in comparison to the odds of the second group[2]		Comparator
Study characteristics	**Full time**	**Part time**	
Following a course in a higher education institution	1.43	–	Registered with a higher education institution but following a course in a further education college
Registered with a higher education institution but following a course in a further education college	–	1.56	Following a course in a higher education institution
Moving onto another higher education course having succeeded in obtaining a foundation degree (which usually allows entry to the first degree at year 2 or beyond)	1.32	1.91	Without having followed a foundation degree course
Not following a strategically important science, technology, engineering or maths course	1.19	1.20	On a strategically important science, technology, engineering or maths course
Not following a modern foreign language course	1.44	No more or less	On a modern foreign language course
Personal characteristics			
With three As at A level or equivalents	2.21	1.49	With two Ds at A level or equivalents
Women	1.30	1.11	Men
18 year olds	1.23	–	20 year olds[3]
From home areas with the highest rates of participation	1.19	1.07	From home areas with the lowest rates of participation
Socio-economic classifications 1–3 ('middle class')	1.10	1.30	Socio-economic classifications 4–7 ('working class')[4]
Chinese or Indian	1.20	–	White
White	–	1.11	Chinese or Indian
Pakistani or Bangladeshi	1.09	–	White
White	–	1.24	Pakistani or Bangladeshi
With a declared disability	1.05	1.11	With no declared disability

Source: National Audit Office analysis of Higher Education Statistics Agency student data

NOTES

1 This table shows statistically significant associations between continuation and selected characteristics from the Higher Education Statistics Agency student data for full-time and part-time undergraduates, including those of the Open University. The model used to generate these results does not take account of characteristics that could make a difference to retention but for which there is no reliable national data, for example on institutions' support systems and student characteristics such as whether they have taken a 'gap year'. In addition, it is not possible to include every characteristic, but if other different characteristics were included in the model it is possible that some of the associations shown above could change. The model also does not take account of part-time students being more likely to follow their courses on a flexible, and therefore interrupted pathway, and are more likely to have breaks in their studies which will contribute to their continuation rates being lower.

2 These are the statistically significant 'odds ratios', which compare the probabilities of continuation for two groups of students whilst other characteristics remain constant. An odds ratio of 1.00 indicates that continuation is equally likely in both groups of student. An odds ratio greater than 1.00 indicates that continuation is more likely in the first group. For example, the chances of a full-time female student continuing are 91.6 to 8.4; those of a male student 89.4 to 10.6. The odds ratio is therefore: 91.6 ÷ 8.4 = 10.9 (students that continue for every one that leaves early) divided by 89.4 ÷ 10.6 = 8.4, which equals 1.3. See Appendix 4 for further details of the model.

3 The effect on continuation of a student's age when the student is over 21 years is minimal.

4 Socio-economic groups 4–7: Small employers and own account workers, Lower supervisory and technical occupations, Semi-routine occupations, Routine occupations.

1.27 The performance indicators published by the Higher Education Statistics Agency exclude students who leave before December each year. This is because the Funding Council considers that reasons for leaving very early are often unrelated to the institution. Consequently around 6,700 early leavers are not reflected in the statistics (which would be equivalent to 2.4 percentage points on the reported non-continuation rate for 2004-05).[25]

The reasons for non-completion have been researched

1.28 Extensive research has been carried out into reasons for voluntary withdrawal. These include the National Audit Office research of 2002 and research at national and institutional level. The most commonly cited reasons for withdrawal are:

- personal reasons;
- lack of integration;
- dissatisfaction with course/institution;
- lack of preparedness;
- wrong choice of course;
- financial reasons; and
- to take up a more attractive opportunity.

More detailed reasons are set out in Appendix 3. In addition, some students fail their assessments, are excluded or take an intermediate qualification rather than proceed with their original course. Examples from our survey of early leavers are shown in **Figure 17**.

1.29 Institutions can respond appropriately if they have good information on the reasons and timing of withdrawal. The Higher Education Statistics Agency collects a reason for leaving for all early leavers from higher education providers which shows that few instances of academic failure are identified before the summer term. It is during the summer term that some students accept an intermediate qualification rather than continue with their original course. The Funding Council does not use the reason for leaving data as it considers that it is not sufficiently robust. In addition, the Higher Education Statistics Agency allows only one reason for withdrawal to be recorded, whereas more in-depth research has suggested that many students leave for a combination of reasons.

17 Examples of early leavers

Leaving early because a new opportunity arose

P chose his university because he had heard good things about the city. He had felt a degree would stand him in good stead for the future, but as his studies progressed he decided that he wanted to be a martial arts instructor. He did not feel the need to continue his course and made a positive choice to leave when an opportunity arose.

Financial pressure

L was a mature student, studying for a degree in the evenings at her local university while she continued to work full time. She was supporting two children. When L found out that she was not eligible for a grant or loan herself as her income was too high, she decided not to continue. L plans to re-start her studies once her children are older.

Poor choice of course

G was a full-time science student, at a university recommended by his school. He found the first year much harder work than he had expected, and he had not realised the requirement to attend all laboratory sessions to pass the course or that the course included a physics element. He left after failing the first year, and intends to study a different subject at another institution.

A difficult decision to leave

M was a mature student studying at a university near home. Following a serious car accident she took a three-year leave of absence. Though the university was very supportive when she returned, M found that the course content had moved on and she withdrew as she expected to fail the exams. Because she felt that she had let everyone down, she did not consult anyone at the university about her decision to leave.

Transferring between institutions

Q chose her university because of its reputation. However, after the first few weeks the course was not meeting her expectations which were based on pre-course reading material. She also found her personal tutor unsupportive. Having made enquiries at another university, which she found very helpful, she transferred.

Source: National Audit Office telephone survey of early leavers

25 Based on National Audit Office analysis of the Higher Education Statistics Agency's student data and performance indicators.

PART TWO

The Funding Council's role

2.1 This part of the report covers:

- the roles of the Department and the Funding Council in overseeing the higher education sector;
- the effect of the Funding Council's funding arrangements on institutions, including those with poor records for retention;
- the publication of performance infomation; and
- the role of the Funding Council and other public bodies in sharing good practice.

The Funding Council oversees autonomous institutions

2.2 The Department for Innovation, Universities and Skills has overall responsibility for public spending in higher education in England and setting the overall policy direction. It has delegated day-to-day responsibility to the Funding Council to account for the proper use of public money, and to provide assurance that the higher education sector is managed effectively and that value for money is being achieved. **Figure 18** provides further details on their respective responsibilities.

2.3 The Funding Council works in partnership with institutions as an enabler, encouraging the sector to achieve the government's strategic objectives primarily through funding incentives and the publication of performance information. This approach recognises institutions as autonomous bodies that are legally independent of government, and preserves their academic freedom. According to the Higher Education Policy Institute,[26] these arrangements have 'contributed to the dynamism, vibrancy and quality of our higher education system'.[27] Compared with many other countries, the Funding Council is less closely involved in institutions' activities. Where an institution's performance gives rise to concern, the Funding Council's regional team makes contact with the institution. It considers that it has strong, open and mutually supportive relationships with institutions, a viewpoint confirmed in most of our interviews with senior managers of institutions.

The funding regime provides incentives to improve retention

2.4 A key element of the sector's income is Funding Council grants, which totalled £6.7 billion in the 2006-07 academic year, including £4.2 billion for teaching funds. Although the Funding Council calculates teaching funds according to student numbers in academic departments, the funding is intended to support institutions generally including, for example, central facilities such as student services, libraries and activities related to the retention of students. Institutions have considerable freedom in how they distribute funds internally to support their aims and objectives, so long as they comply with the conditions of grant. The Funding Council intends that its funding mechanism provides performance incentives to institutions while minimising the accountability burden.

26 The Higher Education Policy Institute is a research organisation, established in 2002 with a grant from the Funding Council. Now largely self-financing, its key function is to raise and research policy issues, stimulate discussion and disseminate its own and others' research findings.
27 Bekhradnia B (2004) *Government, Funding Council and Universities: How should they relate?*, Higher Education Policy Institute.

2.5 The Funding Council's initial allocation of most of the teaching grant reflects an institution's student numbers in the previous year, plus an additional amount for any allocated growth in student numbers awarded to the institution and/or a reduction for under-recruitment in the previous year. If the numbers of students actually completing the year and/or their mix between different subjects or modes of study vary from what is expected then the Funding Council may hold back part of the grant. This holdback occurs when the total funding (plus an assumption for income from tuition fees, based on sector-wide rates) allocated to the institution is more than five per cent above the amount that the pattern of completing students justifies. Changes in the numbers of some types of "more expensive" student, such as those on laboratory-based courses, has more effect than other types: in 2006-07, the basic rate of grant funding ranged from £2,521 to £13,684 per full-time student, depending on the type of course taken.

2.6 The Funding Council applies hold back of funding in-year, and can also reduce an institution's grant for the following year by an equivalent amount. However, the institution can recover funding reduced for the following year if it makes good its position by, for example, having more students complete the year of study (which may be achieved by increased recruitment or better retention).

2.7 The Funding Council does not adjust the levels of teaching grant on the basis of institutions' performance indicators. However, an institution's under-performance against its continuation benchmark may be indicative of a lower than expected rate of students completing their year of study, which may itself lead to a funding adjustment. We therefore looked at the Funding Council's grant allocations to six institutions that had substantially under-performed against their benchmarks[28] for student retention for at least three consecutive years up to 2003-04.[29] The Funding Council withheld some funding from five of these institutions on at least one occasion during the period 2003-04 to 2005-06.

- Four of the five institutions lost funding ranging from £730,000 to £1.3 million because they had not achieved the agreed increases in student numbers; and on average the institutions recovered a little over 40 per cent of this funding by increasing student completions (of year) in the next academic year.
- Two of the five institutions lost funding (£4 million in one case and £200,000 in the other) because their funding would otherwise have exceeded, by more than five per cent, what was justified by their overall level of teaching activity (whether due to problems in recruitment or retention of students or both). Neither institution regained this funding in the subsequent year.

18 Government responsibilities for higher education in England

- The Department for Innovation, Universities and Skills has overall responsibililty for public spending in higher education in England. It develops the Government's higher education policy and sets national targets. The Department's key objective is to raise and widen participation in higher education of 18 to 30 year olds. The Government's target is: to increase participation in higher education by 2010 towards 50 per cent and also make significant progress year-on-year towards fair access, and bear down on rates of non-completion. The Department, through the Secretary of State, is accountable to Parliament for the activities and performance of the Funding Council and provides funding and guidance on priorities to the Funding Council in an annual grant letter.
- The Funding Council is a non-departmental public body set up in 1992 that works at arm's-length from government within an agreed policy and financial framework. It is a relatively small organisation, with around 240 staff, and administration costs of £18 million a year. It distributes public funding for higher education and has key roles in developing and implementing policy, identifying and disseminating good practice and, through part-funding of the independent Quality Assurance Agency for Higher Education, for assessing the quality of learning and teaching.
- Members of the Funding Council's Board, including the Chairman, are appointed by the Secretary of State. The Board provides strategic direction and takes advice from five Committees structured around the Funding Council's four core strategic aims: learning and teaching; widening participation and fair access; research; the contribution of higher education to the economy and society; as well as one committee that looks at leadership, governance and management.
- One of the Funding Council's 22 key performance targets is to maintain or improve the proportion of full-time, first-degree students at English higher education institutions who continue into their second year, compared with 2002-03 (paragraph 1.9). Sector performance against the target is periodically considered by both the Widening Participation Advisory Committee and its Quality, Learning and Teaching Advisory Committee, and the Board receives regular updates on developments.

Source: National Audit Office

28 There will always be a proportion of institutions achieving below their benchmark, because the benchmarks are calculated from sector averages.
29 These six institutions were at least two percentage points below their benchmark in each of 2001-02, 2002-03 and 2003-04.

2.8 We also examined how many institutions were affected by hold back of funding. In 2003-04, the Funding Council held back funding from 33 institutions. For 12 of these institutions that had funding held back due to a fall in student numbers, seven improved their retention performance in 2004-05 but five did not.

Funding to support widening participation and retention activities

2.9 The National Audit Office report *Widening participation in higher education in England* (2002) recommended that the Funding Council review the funding for teaching mature and part-time students and for widening participation activities to make adequate allowance for cost variations between institutions. The Funding Council commissioned J M Consulting Ltd in 2003 to identify the costs of widening participation in higher education. From 18 case studies, the consultants estimated that the additional cost per widening participation student was around £900 on average.[30]

2.10 For a more equitable distribution of funding across the sector and to counteract disincentives that the teaching fund allocation method might have on institutions enrolling widening participation students, in 1999-2000 the Funding Council introduced a new funding stream, the 'widening participation element'. A minority of the teaching grant has since been annually allocated to institutions based on the mix of students they enrol, with the aim of widening access. From 2003-04, the Funding Council substantially increased this recurrent funding by introducing another element with the aim of improving retention, particularly among the types of students who are more difficult to retain. This new element was financed by a reduction in the rest of the teaching grant. The Funding Council's main purpose for the funding was to remove a disincentive to recruit students who may be more likely to leave early. In 2006-07, the Funding Council allocated £345 million to institutions through this funding, around eight per cent of the total teaching grant, which consisted of:

- £240 million for improving retention (including £184 million based on numbers of full-time students in risk categories associated with entry qualifications and age, and £56 million based on numbers of part-time students);
- £92 million based on the prevalence of students living in areas with low rates of participation in higher education or on the average educational achievements of their home areas; and
- £13 million based on the numbers of students in receipt of Disabled Students' Allowances.

2.11 In financial terms, the introduction of the improving retention allocation in 2003-04 meant some institutions gained while others lost: this is because it was a redistribution of existing funding rather than a new stream of funding. We examined institutions' student continuation rates in relation to their benchmarks after their funding was adjusted for the types of students they had enrolled. However, the results were inconclusive.

2.12 The Funding Council does not require institutions to keep records on the use or impact of their widening participation grant because it is part of the teaching grant. Until 2003-04, this element of funding was conditional upon the institutions providing acceptable strategies and action plans. Under the Higher Education Act 2004, institutions choosing to vary their tuition fees must submit access agreements to the new Office for Fair Access (paragraph 2.21). In order to minimise the administrative burden on institutions, the Funding Council withdrew its requirement for strategies and action plans. Most institutions we visited spent their grant as part of their whole budget, although Aston University could account for it in detail **(Figure 19)**.

19 Aston University's distribution of the widening participation grant 2006-07

Aston University has detailed information on the cost of its widening participation and retention work.

	£000
Outreach and widening participation (including staffing, language courses, summer schools, performance monitoring)	428
Academic support (including learning support centre, maths support centre)	313
Supporting students with disabilities (including disability unit, adjustments)	176
Placements and employability (including careers advice, student job shop)	126
Other initiatives (including welfare support, peer mentoring)	71
Total	**1,114**

Source: Aston University

30 J M Consulting Ltd (an independent firm specialising in public sector reviews), 2004, *The costs of widening participation in higher education*.

Publication of performance information encourages performance improvement

2.13 Annual performance indicators for institutions are published by the Higher Education Statistics Agency. The indicators are intended to provide reliable and comparable information for a range of users, including prospective students, institutions and the Funding Council. The users, through the Performance Indicators Steering Group, oversee the development of the indicators. The retention indicators are published two years after the end of the academic year covered, because some indicators require information from the subsequent year which then needs to be prepared for publication. The Higher Education Statistics Agency, in conjunction with the Steering Group, is considering the scope for bringing forward publication of the retention indicators by several months. The publication of the indicators allows an institution's record on retention to be compared with the higher education sector as a whole, and against other institutions.

2.14 Publication of performance information provides an incentive to institutions to perform well. In part, this is because the media uses the information to create 'league tables' of institutions. The indicators can affect institutions' reputations and numbers of student applications. However, there are two main areas where the indicators are incomplete: they exclude part-time students and they exclude first-year students who leave before December.

2.15 There are some difficulties in interpreting data on part-time students because, for example, part-time study can be intentionally intermittent. However, when the Funding Council introduced the indicators, it noted that it would be looking for a way to include part-time students. Since 1998-99 the (full-time equivalent) number of part-time students has increased by 40 per cent compared with a 17 per cent increase in full-time students, and credit-based courses (which are often taken by part-time students) have become more important.[31] In a recent consultation exercise, a number of institutions expressed an interest in the development of retention indicators for part-time students.[32] Some countries, such as Australia, already publish such performance indicators and the Higher Education Statistics Agency's indicators for Welsh universities include module completion rates.

2.16 The exclusion from the indicators of students who leave before December in their first year means that the indicators do not represent a true picture of student retention and under-state non-continuation in most institutions. These leavers are excluded because the Funding Council considers they often leave for reasons unrelated to the institution, and it also provides the flexibility for a student to 'try out' higher education, courses and institutions without the institution being penalised if the student leaves early.

2.17 Performance indicators together with other information, particularly when presented in league table format, can influence potential students' selection of an institution, and possibly even their decision whether to enter higher education. The Committee of Public Accounts concluded in 2002 that there was a need to improve information for potential students.[33] There is now more information available: in 2004, the Department and the Funding Council launched the Aimhigher and Teaching Quality Information websites.[34] The Aimhigher website is targeted in particular at potential students from non-traditional backgrounds, and has been the more heavily used: between January and May 2006 it averaged 110,000 'unique visitors' per month, while the Teaching Quality Information website averaged only 19,000 unique visitors. By comparison, there were 506,000 applicants for places starting in 2006, implying that the Teaching Quality Information website is under-used. The Funding Council has let a contract to redesign and re-launch this website, with the aim of doubling usage.[35]

2.18 Students' views are a key source of information on the quality of institutions. Since 2005, the Funding Council has commissioned a National Student Survey, at a cost of £1.5 million annually. In 2006, the Survey achieved a 56 per cent response rate from mainly final year students, and the results showed an overall course satisfaction of around 80 per cent. This response rate allows reliable analysis of responses by subject and by institution for either full-time or part-time students. The detailed results are published on the Teaching Quality Information website for potential students. Institutions that we visited also find it helpful in benchmarking their performance, and stakeholders generally think highly of the Survey. A sector review group reported that institutions had mixed views about the Survey, but they took the results seriously and made changes as a result.[36]

31 National Audit Office analysis of Higher Education Statistics Agency student data.
32 Higher Education Funding Council for England (2007), *Review of performance indicators: Outcomes and decisions*, www.hefce.ac.uk/pubs/hefce/2007/07_14/.
33 Committee of Public Accounts, 58th Report 2001-02, *Improving Student Achievement and Widening Participation in Higher Education in England* (the relevant recommendations are reproduced at Appendix 5).
34 www.aimhigher.ac.uk and www.tqi.ac.uk. Aimhigher was originally launched in September 2001 as 'Excellence Challenge' and became Aimhigher in August 2004, after joining the Funding Council and Learning and Skills Council-led university outreach programme Partnerships for Progression.
35 Website usage statistics provided by the Funding Council.
36 Quality Assurance Framework Review Group (2006), *Review of the quality assurance framework: phase 2 outcomes*.

The Funding Council and other public bodies encourage the sharing of good practice

2.19 Effective teaching and learning enhances the student experience and can contribute to good retention.[37] One of the main Funding Council programmes that helps develop and share good practice in this area is the Centres for Excellence in Teaching and Learning. The overall aim of this programme is to reward excellence and encourage its dissemination across the sector. In January 2005, the Funding Council approved funding for 74 Centres of Excellence, based in institutions, two of which particularly emphasise retention. In total, the Centres will receive £291 million of additional funding from 2005-06 to 2009-10 for teaching and learning projects and are required to provide annual returns on progress against their objectives. The Funding Council plans to complete an evaluation of the programme in 2010.

2.20 The Funding Council also funds four other bodies that contribute to the dissemination of good practice.

- The Quality Assurance Agency for Higher Education is the independent body responsible for safeguarding the public interest in standards in higher education qualifications and for encouraging continuous improvement in the management of the quality of higher education. In addition to a variety of other activities undertaken across the United Kingdom, the Agency carries out and publishes reports of institutional audits of all institutions in England on a six-year cycle. Although the reports focus primarily on academic activities, they often also cover support services and highlight examples of good practice, including activities to improve retention. The Agency spent £11 million in 2005-06, of which about £4 million came from the Funding Council.
- The Higher Education Academy supports the enhancement of the student learning experience in higher education and works at sector, institutional, discipline and individual staff levels to do this, including by supporting the Centres for Excellence in Teaching and Learning. The Academy received £17 million in Funding Council grants in 2005-06.
- Action on Access is the national coordination team for widening participation in higher education. It provides advice to practitioners and policy makers including its funders: the Funding Council and the Department for Employment and Learning in Northern Ireland. It also supports the sector, through dissemination events, conferences, e-bulletins and publications on widening participation. The team produced a review of student retention and performance indicators from 1999 to 2003, which identified issues and raised policy questions, and was aimed at helping institutions use their own performance indicator data effectively.[38] The cost of running Action on Access was £855,000 in 2006-07.
- The Equality Challenge Unit was established in 2001 and covers a wide range of equality and diversity issues for students and staff. Action on Access, the Academy and the Unit work together in the Disability Equality Partnership, which is responsible for providing support to institutions in the form of briefings, resources, guidance, events and bespoke advice about supporting students with disabilities. In addition, the Disability Rights Commission provides institutions with a number of guides to their duties and a code of practice, as well as exercising its enforcement role.

2.21 The Office for Fair Access was set up in 2004 with the primary aim of increasing applications and entrants from low income and other under-represented groups following the introduction of variable tuition fees in 2006-07. It requires all institutions charging tuition fees above the basic amount to have an approved access agreement that sets out their measures for promoting and safeguarding fair access, primarily the provision of bursaries and scholarships, and some 'outreach' activity. Although these agreements are not focused primarily on retention, the types of students included in fair access are often those who are more likely to not complete their course. It may therefore be helpful for institutions to set out their objectives for retention, although they are not required to do so and not all institutions have a retention issue to address. We found that 36 of the 124 institutions with an access agreement chose to include a retention target. Often, though, the targets could have been defined in a way that would enable more effective performance measurement. The Office monitors institutions' annual progress towards their access agreement targets. During 2009, an independent commission will evaluate the impact of access agreements which is likely to require early evidence on the relationship between bursaries and retention.

2.22 The range of activities described above contributes to the spread of good practice on retention, as evidenced by research reports, conferences and informal contacts between institutions. In addition, the Funding Council conducts various other activities that widen knowledge on retention. For example, its analytical services group conducts and publishes research, including on student retention. However, we found only limited firm evidence of the impact of practices on retention, and the evaluation and dissemination of good practices would benefit from being more systematic.

37 Laing, C, and Robinson, A (2003) *The Withdrawal of Non-traditional Students: developing an explanatory model*, Journal of Further and Higher Education, 27, 2.
38 Action on Access (2004), *Student Retention and HEFCE Performance Indicators: Discussion Paper*.

PART THREE

Institutions' approaches to retaining students

3.1 This part of the report examines how institutions can improve their retention of students. Our international review indicated that similar approaches are being used in English institutions and the four countries we considered – the United States, the Netherlands, Republic of Ireland and Australia.

Using management information to understand retention

3.2 Nationally, the types of student who are more likely to be vulnerable to not completing their course are partially understood. However, apart from the much lower retention of part-time students (paragraph 1.23) differences in the characteristics of groups of students are relatively small. Most students who give up their course do so for a range of reasons – personal, institutional and/or course related. It is therefore important that institutions have a good knowledge of their own students' characteristics, progression and achievement and are able to identify specific areas of concern, for example with particular courses or services. Similarly, institutions should have a good knowledge of the factors that contribute to high retention rates.

3.3 Many of the institutions we visited were collating and disseminating information on withdrawal rates, including by ethnicity and disability. This data was being collected as part of the institutions' monitoring of the progress of their students. Most managers considered the information to be essential for good management, and the additional costs of monitoring retention were considered to be modest. Nottingham Trent University, for example, produces monthly monitoring reports to key decision makers. Several of the institutions were tracking attendance and academic achievement of students, in order to highlight those students who may need more support **(Figure 20)**.

3.4 Information on the reasons for withdrawal can help an institution to decide if a response is necessary and take action. Many institutions rely on exit interviews or postal questionnaires, in part to satisfy the Higher Education Statistics Agency's information requirements (paragraph 1.29). Two institutions we visited, Edge Hill University and Nottingham Trent University, had obtained a better understanding by carrying out in-depth research including surveys as well as interviews with early leavers.

20 Tracking and support for vulnerable students – The University of East London

Through its management information system, the University identified an increased risk of losing students who had entered through 'clearing' about a month after the start of term, when first assignments were due and when financial and other concerns can also arise.

In response, the University trained postgraduate and final year students to be support advisers, and had them telephone the students during week four to check how they were doing. Additional capacity was made available in support services, so that all students who wanted to could see support services the next day. The response was positive. For example, 60 extra students attended the money advice centre during the week, and 'crash courses' in study skills were offered. For a cost of approximately £5,000 – the equivalent of the annual fee income of fewer than two students – the University's early evaluation showed an average 1.6 percentage point decrease in the withdrawal rate, and it therefore seems probable that approximately 12 additional students were retained. The University planned to carry out a full evaluation of impact at the end of a full academic year.

The University also monitors the performance of students by module in order to identify modules with high failure rates, which may indicate that learning and teaching or methods of assessment need to be adjusted.

Source: National Audit Office/The University of East London

3.5 In its institutional reviews, the Quality Assurance Agency stresses the importance of collating robust management information to monitor retention and notes that there is scope for improvement.[39] Around half of the institutions covered by the Funding Council's sample audits of 2005-06 student data were found to have inaccurate forecasts or records of non-completion, with potential funding consequences such as claw back.[40] We found that information collated tends to be localised to particular programmes or departments. There is also insufficient evaluation of the cost and effectiveness of retention initiatives in institutions, and in the evaluation that does exist, it can be difficult to separate the impacts of retention-related activity from the impacts of other actions to improve the student experience. Our international research noted a similar lack of evaluation of cost and impact.

Building strategic commitment to retaining students

3.6 Strong senior management commitment can drive institutions to improve the quality of the student experience, retain more students and extend provision to non-traditional students. Institutions with good records for retaining students tend to place a high strategic priority on retention, and communicate this effectively to academic and support staff.

3.7 The pre-1992 institutions we visited tended to see their good performance on student retention as a result of their high standards in recruitment and in learning and teaching. However, research undertaken in 2003 indicated that activities to recruit and retain students, particularly from non-traditional backgrounds, can be regarded as add-ons, rather than as integral to the institution but that there is an increasing commitment by institutions to address this.[41] As an example from one of the institutions we visited, in 2006 the University of Liverpool adopted a new academic strategy that brought together previously separate strategies covering the whole of its learning and teaching, widening participation and retention activities. The post-1992 institutions we visited tended to have strategies specifically for retention, with resources allocated to deliver them **(Figure 21)**, perhaps reflecting the types of students that they recruit. Institutions in the Republic of Ireland and the Netherlands also had resources dedicated specifically to retention, for example retention support officers.

3.8 Most importantly, senior management can use the strategy to emphasise to staff that teaching practice has to respond to changing student needs: "we need to teach the students we recruit, not the ones we would have liked to recruit".[42]

21 A central retention team – The University of Teesside

In 2003 the University received support from the European Social Fund to research retention, which led to the establishment of a central retention team. The team undertakes a range of activities to support retention work across the University, including:

- developing a central retention action plan for departments to use as a framework for their local retention plans;
- co-ordinating retention support officers. These officers offer approachable, school-based support for students, and provide a link between the academic staff and student services. For example, they are responsible for contacting students who are not attending class and, if appropriate, referring them to student services or organising peer support;
- maintaining retention information;
- supporting staff through advice, workshops, written guidance; and
- research work.

The initial grant was for £120,000 and the University now funds the team itself. In 2002-03 the University's continuation rate was 89.7 per cent (2.3 percentage points better than benchmark). In 2004-05 the rate had improved to 90.8 per cent (2.7 percentage points above their updated (higher) benchmark), although it is possible that other factors were involved in the improvement.

Source: National Audit Office/The University of Teesside

39 Quality Assurance Agency (2006) *Outcomes from Institutional Audit: Institutions' Support for Widening Participation and Access to Higher Education.* This paper is based on a review of 70 institutional audit reports published between 2002-03 and 2003-04.

40 Higher Education Funding Council (2006), *Higher Education Students Early Statistics Survey (HESES) 2006-07.* To audit student data returns, the Funding Council uses a risk-based assessment to select institutions for audit visits. Up to 25 institutions are audited each year on a seven year cycle. The risk-based approach means that audit findings and their funding consequences among the sampled institutions may not be representative of the sector as a whole.

41 Layer, Srivastava, Thomas, and Yorke (2003), Student Success: Building for change, in *Student Success in Higher Education*, Action on Access; Higher Education Funding Council (2006), *Widening Participation: A Review*, www.hefce.ac.uk/widen/aimhigh/WPfinalreview.pdf.

42 Anthony Cook, Student Transition and Recruitment (STAR) project, University of Ulster, Universities UK Student Retention and Progression conference, Feb 2007.

Securing commitment from students

3.9 All of the institutions we visited were conscious of the need to provide potential students with accurate information about the courses offered. In Australia, Ireland and the Netherlands, there are examples of institutions experimenting with providing tailored information and support to new students. For example, peer mentoring – whereby second and final year students give informal support to new students – is a feature of the student experience in Ireland, the Netherlands, the United States, and has been tried in several English institutions. Institutions are experimenting with different models of mentoring and believe it helps to build students' engagement with the institution and their course. The University of Aston allocates £8,000 to peer mentoring from its widening participation grant.

3.10 Students who start to miss lectures and tutorials can fall behind and put their chances of completing at risk. Some institutions take attendance registers, at least for smaller classes, and academic staff or faculty administrators follow up non-attendance as part of their normal responsibilities, contacting absent students to enquire into their circumstances, stressing the importance of attendance and, where appropriate, signposting to the support that is available **(Figure 22)**. Other institutions place greater emphasis on independent learning than following up absence.

22 A Student Charter – The University of East London

The University's Student Charter sets out the terms of the relationship between students and the University, describing what can be expected of both parties in a range of areas such as teaching and learning, assessment, and student services. The Student Charter stresses that successful full-time students ought to be studying at university and independently for 35 hours a week and avoid taking breaks during a semester.

The University takes a firm line on unexplained non-attendance: absence on three consecutive occasions for a module, or attendance generally falling below 75 per cent, can lead to a student being deregistered from that module. The University estimates the costs of monitoring attendance through texting and telephoning students at £18,000 a year – equivalent to the fee income from six students.

Source: National Audit Office/The University of East London

Providing support through personal tutoring

3.11 Research has indicated that effective personal tutoring may be an important factor in retaining more students.[43] Most if not all institutions provide students with additional academic support through personal tutoring systems, which allocate students to staff who provide pastoral and sometimes academic support. Students told us that they value this support:

> **"I had a lot of problems at the end of year one and the personal tutor, he was fabulous... they are there to help you."**

3.12 Institutions are, however, facing challenges with their personal tutor systems, and some students have not felt well supported by their personal tutor and are reluctant to see them again. There can be difficulties in defining the precise role of a personal tutor and the acceptable amount of contact time or availability to students. There is sometimes a need for a more structured approach, which is less dependent upon the work schedule or goodwill of individual members of staff, and provides training to tutors so that they know how and when to refer to student services. Several institutions we visited were undertaking a review of their systems.

> **"I think certainly as first year students, we feel a little bit reluctant to maybe go to the personal tutor when we have problems and things just go on the slide a little bit."**

3.13 Academic and financial pressures mean that institutions make use of hourly paid staff such as associate lecturers and postgraduate students to teach some classes. These staff may not be so well placed to provide the level of student contact outside taught sessions that can help identify students in difficulty. Also, research staff have substantial demands on their time outside of teaching. Smaller institutions and colleges can have a more personal and informal environment, in which students and academics have a closer relationship.

43 Davies R and Elias P (2003), *Dropping out: A study of early leavers from higher education*, Department for Education and Skills Research Report 386.

Academic provision

3.14 Effective academic support helps to equip an increasingly diverse student body with the skills necessary to succeed in higher education. Some institutions start early by offering non-traditional students the opportunity to attend pre-entry courses **(Figure 23)**. Transitional courses and skills training were features in all four of the international comparison countries.

3.15 All the institutions we visited provided learning support opportunities for students to improve their academic skills once they had started their course **(Figure 24)**. These opportunities took the form of elective modules (which counted towards the final degree), learning centres, and summer schools for revision. At most of the institutions we visited, students were expected to maintain a personal development plan.

23 Pre-entry courses for non-traditional students – Edge Hill University

For non-traditional students, in this case mature students who have not studied in full-time education for at least three years, the University offers a seven-week full-time course on campus beginning in May or July. Applicants are selected by interview, but the course is free and financial support may be available for travel and childcare. Applicants are trained in subject-specific study skills without needing a longer access course.

Source: National Audit Office/Edge Hill University

24 Study skills for students – Newcastle University

Students are given a 'study skills' folder at the start of the course which sets out how university study differs from study at school or college, and gives hints, tips and checklists on:

- time management, including working independently;
- project planning;
- university teaching methods (the roles of lectures, seminars and tutorials);
- written communication, including referencing and avoiding plagiarism;
- note-taking skills;
- presentation skills; and
- revision techniques.

Source: National Audit Office/Newcastle University

3.16 Many students require some additional academic support, especially in the mathematical skills required in science, mathematics, engineering and technology. Generally, the higher a student's pre-entry qualifications, the higher their chance of success in completing their degree. However, our analysis has found that for full-time students in these technical subjects the difference in continuation between students with high and low entry qualifications is more marked **(Figure 25)**. Institutions are responding by introducing innovative ways of teaching to build students' skills and confidence, such as project-based learning in smaller groups. Institutions in the Netherlands and the United States are creating similar small learning communities. Mathematics drop-in centres are becoming a more common feature in English institutions, and two examples we saw cost around £60,000 to £70,000 a year to operate.

Broadening the options for learning

3.17 Some institutions are amending traditional methods of delivering courses, which could improve the completion chances of their increasingly diverse student population, as their students have more choice of learning options to fit their personal circumstances. Widely used approaches include:

- **Comprehensive modular systems.** The student can accumulate credit over a number of years and not necessarily have to follow a linear route of progression. Groups of institutions in England and Northern Ireland have voluntarily agreed to use the same approach to using credit locally or regionally, which can facilitate the transfer of students. Unlike Scotland and Wales, however, there is no nationally agreed framework.[44] Students may also be able to retrieve previously failed modules in either of the final two years of their degree. In the Netherlands, research has suggested that more flexibility and modularisation of courses can have a positive impact on the retention of students, although research on the United States' experience highlights the risk that increasing flexibility can diminish student integration, as students are less likely to move as a cohort through a course.[45]

44 The report by the Steering Group on Measuring and Recording Student Achievement (the Burgess Report) set out a programme in which all English institutions would voluntarily credit-rate their provision by 2009-10 and thereafter include the credit value in a published description of each programme they offer. Universities UK (2006), *Proposals for national arrangements for the use of academic credit in higher education in England: final report of the Burgess Group.*

45 Lansbergen J (2003), *Literatuurrapport studiestakers en-switchers* (English translation*: Literature review report on students changing/switching courses in higher education and students leaving higher education)*, Fontys Group; Weko T (2004), *New Dogs and Old Tricks: What can the UK teach the US about University Education*, Higher Education Policy Institute.

25 Continuation of students on strategically important science, technology, engineering and mathematics courses

Compared to other subjects, students with lower pre-entry qualifications who study science, technology, engineering or mathematics are on average less likely to continue into a second year.

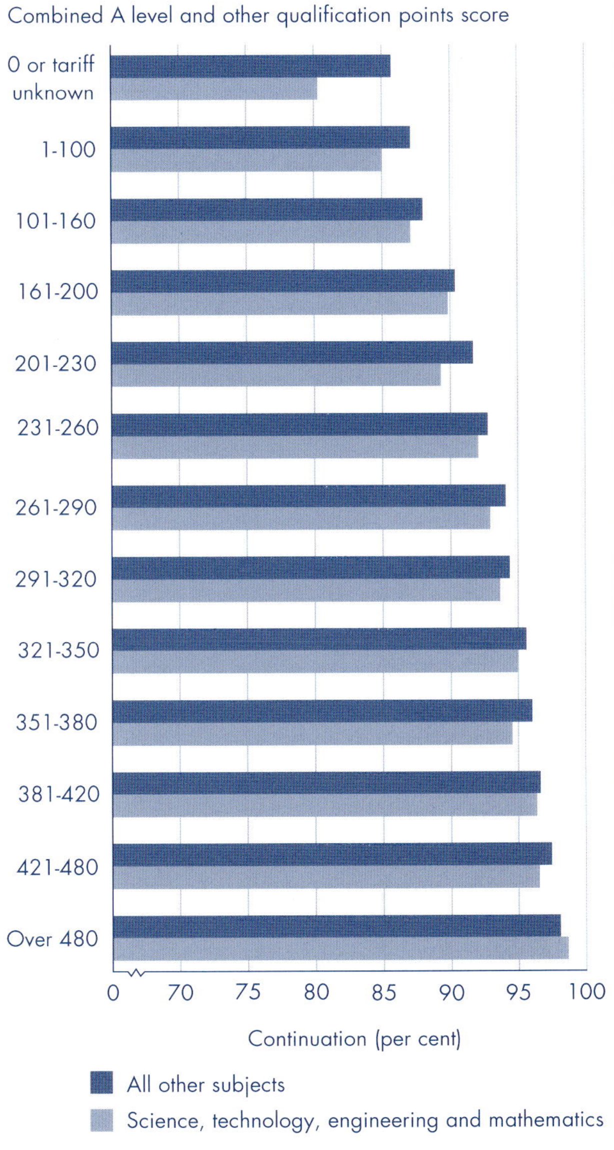

Source: National Audit Office analysis of Higher Education Statistics Agency individual student data

NOTES

1 Based on full-time undergraduates entering in 2004-05.

2 To compare A level grades and achievement in other entry qualifications, UCAS assigns a value to each grade obtained. For A levels, a grade A is worth 120 points, a grade E 40 points.

- **Provision through partner colleges.** Students at institutions we visited were positive about partnership arrangements whereby they could remain at home by basing their studies in a local further education college. Such students felt they benefited from relatively high amounts of contact time with college staff. However, some considered they were not well served by their partner universities in terms of access to central facilities and support services, compared with students who studied and lived on campus full time.
- **Virtual learning.** Institutions use information technology as a tool for learning and providing student feedback, particularly for students who may not be able to physically attend classes. Several of the institutions we visited, for example South Cheshire College and North Lindsey College, made extensive use of the virtual learning environment to monitor the progress of their students, and staff and students at these colleges were positive about the use of technology. Generally though, some academic staff see it as more challenging to assess students' learning needs in this way.
- **The academic calendar.** During our visits we saw examples of institutions which have changed their academic calendar to better reflect their students' circumstances. Examples include starting classes later in the day, teaching in two or three-day blocks, running the same courses on a shift basis during the day and evening, shortening the Christmas break and offering a February start date as an alternative to the traditional September start.

Providing specialist support

3.18 Institutions with student services that are effective and have good links with the rest of the institution tend to be good at retaining students. In the past, student services were sometimes regarded as 'remedial' services, picking up cases only after problems arose. In the institutions we visited, they generally acted proactively, and worked well with academic staff. Institutions can spend substantial sums on student services: for example, the University of East London spends approximately £1.6 million a year in providing student services, excluding its grant to the student union. Many institutions fund their student union to provide support, especially on sensitive issues, and for independent advocacy if the student is in dispute with the university.

3.19 Some institutions are centralising their support services, creating a 'one-stop shop', to facilitate student access and improve the quality of the student experience. It is difficult to assess the impact of this change, because the quality of student services is not routinely assessed by the Quality Assurance Agency. Institutions are gaining accreditation using other quality measures, including the matrix quality Standard for information, advice and guidance services and Investors in People.[46] The national representative organisation, the Association of Managers of Student Services in Higher Education, is looking to develop performance measures to enable benchmarking.

Financial support

3.20 From 2006-07, the arrangements for tuition fees were changed. Full-time undergraduates in England starting their courses from 2006-07 typically pay tuition fees of £3,000 a year.[47] Institutions charging such fees must set up bursary schemes for students from low income families, and low interest loans are still available to all students in addition to maintenance grants for students from low income families. It is too early to assess the impact of these changes on retention. Many institutions we visited were aware that students rely on part-time work to ease financial pressures and the student unions play a role in offering 'job shops' which only advertise positions with appropriate pay, hours and terms and conditions.

3.21 Research on specific bursary schemes in place before 2006-07 suggests that they may improve retention: they can reduce levels of debt and ease transition into higher education, and they can also reinforce the recipient's perception of the institution's commitment to them.[48] Institutions may use the criteria for, and timing of, bursaries to encourage students to progress. For example, the University of East London pays bursaries at enrolment plus a £500 bursary to students progressing to the second semester. London South Bank University pays students £250 graduation bonus in addition to the bursary. In Scotland, students are to be paid on a monthly basis from 2007-08 in order to help with students' budgeting.

3.22 In some of the institutions we visited, fewer students than expected had taken up the new bursaries. Finance officers considered that, for means-tested bursaries, the lower than expected take-up was in part due to potential recipients mistakenly not permitting details of their parental income to be shared (by not ticking the necessary box on the Student Loans Company forms).
For other bursaries, some students may not be aware of the support available.

Support for students with disabilities

3.23 The number of students with declared disabilities entering higher education has increased by just over two-thirds in six years. In total, around 138,000 students declared a disability in 2005-06, up from 82,000 in 2000-01.[49] Looking specifically at new entrants, around 45,000 United Kingdom students with a disability started full and part-time undergraduate courses in 2005-06.[50] The most commonly declared disability is dyslexia: according to Higher Education Statistics Agency data, 54 per cent of full-time students with a disability have dyslexia, compared with 23 per cent of part-time students with a disability.

3.24 Disabled Students' Allowances provide financial help for equipment, non-medical helpers, travel and incidentals that students with a disability often need. They are not, however, intended to cover disability-related expenditure that a person would incur even if they were not attending a higher education course, or any course-related costs not connected with their disability. The Allowances are needs-based and not means-tested, and in 2005-06 £69 million was distributed to full-time, and £4 million to part-time undergraduates. Not every student who describes themselves as having a disability will need the Allowances.

46 The matrix Standard is a national quality standard for any organisation that delivers information, advice and/or guidance on learning and work.

47 The maximum limit for tuition fees for 2006-07 is £3,000 (£3,070 in 2007-08). Most higher education institutions charged this amount, but further education colleges charged less in 2006-07.

48 Emmerson C, Frayne C, McNally S and Silva O (2005) *Economic Evaluation of Opportunity Bursaries, Evaluation of Aimhigher: Excellence Challenge*, Department for Education and Skills; Hatt S, Hannan A, Baxter A, and Harrison N, (2005) "Opportunity Knocks? The impact of bursary schemes on students from low-income backgrounds" in *Studies in Higher Education*, Vol 30 No 4pp373-388; Hatt S, Hannan A, and Baxter A, (2005) "Bursaries and Student Success: A study of students from low income groups at two institutions in the South West" in *Higher Education Quarterly*, Vol 59 No 2pp111-126; Harrison N, Baxter A and Hatt S (2006) *From Opportunity to OFFA: the implementation of discretionary bursaries in the UK and their impact on student finance, academic success and perceptions of institutional habitas*, Unpublished.

49 Higher Education Statistics Agency press release 110 (www.hesa.ac.uk/press/pr110/pr110.htm).

50 Higher Education Statistics Agency: *Resources of Higher Education Institutions 2005-06* Table 11b – First year UK domiciled HE students by qualification aim, mode of study, gender and disability 2005-06 (http://www.hesa.ac.uk/holisdocs/pubinfo/student/disab0506.htm).

3.25 Access to the Allowances improves the continuation chances of both full and part-time students. Disabled students who obtain the Allowances are more likely to continue than both students declaring a disability who do not receive it and students without any disability **(Figure 26)**. This may partly be because students who persevere with applications for the Allowances may also be more likely to persist with their course.

3.26 Although obtaining the Allowances is important to continuation for part-time students, relatively few get them. To qualify for the Allowances, part-time students must be on courses which take no more than twice as long to complete as the full-time equivalent.[51] Our calculations suggest that only 20 per cent of part-time undergraduates with a declared disability who may be eligible (i.e. studying at 50 per cent or more of the full-time equivalent) actually receive the Allowances, compared with 40 per cent of full-time students, though average payments to full and part-time students are similar.[52] There are also substantial variations between institutions in the proportion of students with a declared disability receiving the Allowances **(Figure 27 overleaf)**.

3.27 Institutions reported difficulties in getting their students through the application process for the Allowances. They can have to deal with high numbers of applicants and experience delays in accessing qualified assessors to verify students' disabilities. It is common for university staff to be the first to spot that a student has a specific learning difficulty such as dyslexia, making it difficult to avoid delays caused by a high administrative workload in the first term. Aston University encourages future students to identify their disability, where possible, before enrolment, and then works with them to organise financial and other support in time for the start of term. Newcastle University has a joint disability assessment centre with Durham University.

26 The relationship between Disabled Students' Allowances and continuation rates, 2004-05

Access to Disabled Students' Allowances (DSA) are associated with better rates of continuation.

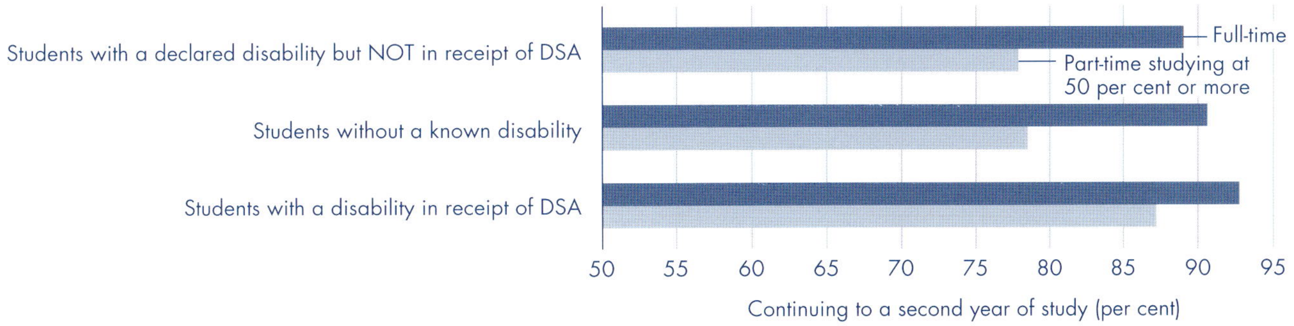

Source: National Audit Office analysis of Higher Education Statistics Agency student data

NOTES

1 The analysis is based on all undergraduate students.

2 The definition of disability is a self-reported assessment by the student, and may not have been independently assessed.

51 On average, part-time, first-degree students study at 47 per cent of full-time equivalent, and all part-time students (including postgraduates) study at around 37 per cent of full-time equivalent – Universities UK (2006) *Part-time students in higher education – supporting higher-level skills and lifelong learning*.

52 Data on total payments and claimants in 2005-06 was supplied by the Department for Innovation, Universities and Skills.

27 Receipt of Disabled Students' Allowances, by institution, 2004-05

Students in some institutions are much more likely to be receiving the Disabled Students' Allowances than in others.

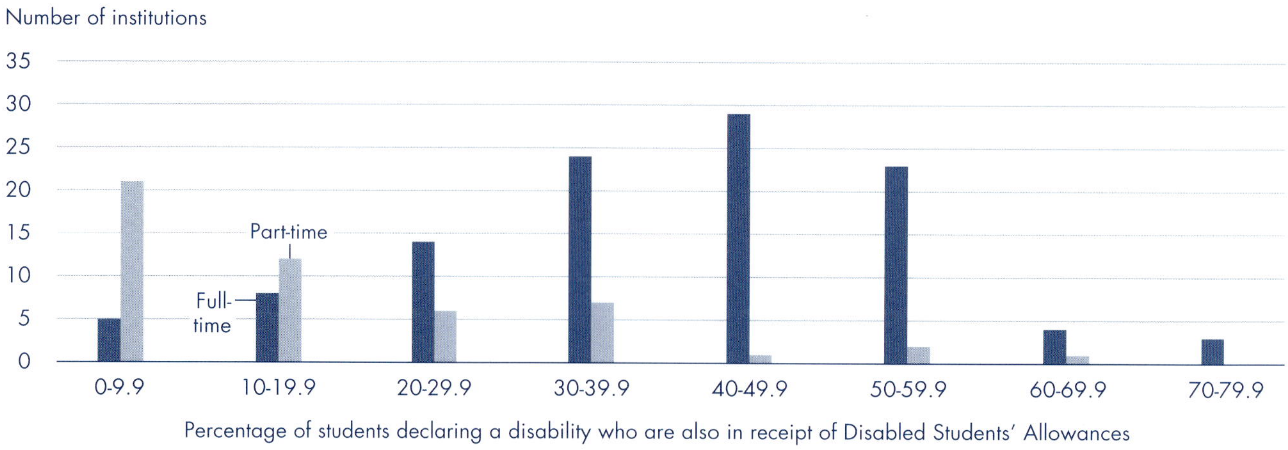

Source: National Audit Office analysis of Higher Education Statistics Agency student data

NOTES

1 This is based on 110 English institutions with 20 or more full-time undergraduates declaring a disability, and 50 English institutions with 20 or more part-time undergraduates declaring a disability studying at 50 per cent or more of the full-time equivalent course.

2 The definition of disability is a self-reported assessment by the student, and may not have been independently assessed.

APPENDIX ONE

Study methodology

1 This report is based on:

- analyses of the Higher Education Statistics Agency's student data and quantitative analyses of higher education performance indicators;
- case studies of selected higher education institutions including a telephone survey of early leavers;
- review of academic and other research;
- international comparison research; and
- consultation with stakeholder groups, reference to experts and discussions with staff of the Department for Innovation, Universities and Skills and the Higher Education Funding Council for England.

Data analysis

2 Our main data source was the Higher Education Statistics Agency's 'Individual Student Record' which holds information on all students funded by the Funding Council who were enrolled on higher education courses with higher education institutions. It includes students registered with a higher education institution and that are taking some or all of their course in a further education college, but not those for whom the Funding Council pays the further education colleges direct.

3 The analysis was conducted by the National Audit Office and reviewed by the Funding Council's analytical team. It included a logistic regression analysis of the student data and a linear regression of institution data. These techniques allowed us to see how inter-relationships between the many characteristics of institutions and students influence likelihood of continuation in higher education.

Evaluative case studies with institutions and colleges

4 We visited eight universities and four further education colleges providing higher education courses. Most of these institutions were selected because their retention of students was improving compared with their benchmarks:

- Aston University;
- University of Bath;
- University of East London;
- Edge Hill University;
- University of Liverpool;
- Macclesfield College (as part of the Macclesfield Consortium recognised by the Funding Council for funding purposes);
- Mid Cheshire College (as part of the Macclesfield Consortium);
- Newcastle University;
- North Lindsey College;
- Nottingham Trent University;
- South Cheshire College (as part of the Macclesfield Consortium); and
- University of Teesside.

5 Our case study visits lasted between one and three days. During the visits, we conducted on average 10 interviews and focus groups with a range of students and staff, including practitioners in welfare services, staff with teaching or pastoral responsibilities, admissions staff, and the Vice Chancellor, Principal or other member of the senior team.

6 The case studies allowed us to explore the relationship between retention and institutional practice in recruitment onto higher education courses, during induction and throughout the course.

7 As part of this work, we also conducted telephone or face-to-face, semi-structured interviews with 17 students who had left their courses early during 2004-05. Our sample came from seven of our case study institutions and included a range of types of student. Many other students we tried to contact had moved or changed their telephone numbers. The interviews helped us to assess the impact that pre-entry advice and information, the clearing system, induction processes and on-going support in institutions had on their decisions about leaving their course. Edge

Hill University supplied us with their own recent research with early leavers and Nottingham Trent University shared initial survey responses from an exploratory study.

8 We also identified several institutions that had substantially under-performed against their benchmarks for student retention for at least three consecutive years up to 2003-04. We reviewed the action taken by the Funding Council to encourage such institutions to improve their performance, including consulting with the Funding Council's lead contacts and senior managers at a sample of the institutions.

Literature review

9 The study team examined published accounts, annual reports, departmental research, policy papers and existing literature on student retention. The work allowed us to obtain a detailed understanding of developments in higher education.

International comparisons

10 We commissioned RAND Europe to compare practice and identify lessons from the higher education system in the Republic of Ireland, the Netherlands, the United States of America and Australia. The comparison countries were selected because of the availability of data and information on student retention, their generally positive trends in the development of student retention rates over time, and/or evidence of interesting or innovative practice in maximising the likelihood of retention in higher education courses.

11 The main output from this element of the research was a written report describing detailed examples of innovative and good practice, from which transferable lessons for the United Kingdom could be drawn. In establishing which examples are good or innovative, the contractor described the national higher education system, evaluated the context, explained the differences in completion rates, described approaches to increase retention which have been tried and evaluated the evidence of the success of these policies. This report, *'Student Retention in Higher Education Courses: International Comparisons'*, is published separately and can be found on our website at www.nao.org.uk.

12 We also contacted representatives in the Higher Education funding bodies of the other home nations to get an overview of the issues affecting student retention in these nations and to identify more qualitative information on institutional practice. These bodies are Northern Ireland's Department for Employment and Learning, the Higher Education Funding Council for Wales and the Scottish Funding Council.

Consulting with experts in the field

13 We used experts to consider the emerging findings from our work and help shape our report and recommendations. They were: Mr Neil Harrison, a student support practitioner from the University of the West of England, and to gain an academic perspective, Dr Diane Nutt from the University of Teesside.

14 During the whole of the study we have interviewed central and regional staff of the Funding Council to examine the coverage of student retention issues across all of its statutory responsibilities, including regulatory activities, funding awards, evaluation and research, and dissemination of good practice.

15 In the course of the study we consulted with experts in the field as well as representatives from the following stakeholder groups and independent bodies:

- Action on Access;
- The Association of Managers of Student Services in Higher Education;
- Association of Colleges;
- Brightside Trust (provider of e-mentoring schemes for disadvantaged students);
- GuildHE;
- National Union of Students;
- Office for Fair Access;
- Office of the Independent Adjudicator for Higher Education;
- Other universities: University of Leicester, London Metropolitan University, London South Bank University, North East Wales Institute of Higher Education, University of Sheffield, Sheffield Hallam University;
- Quality Assurance Agency;
- Researchers: Dr Anthony Cook (University of Ulster), Mr Neil Harrison (University of West of England), Professor John Storan (University of East London), Professor Jocey Quinn (Institute for Policy Studies in Education, London Metropolitan University), Professor Mantz Yorke (Visiting Professor, Department of Educational Research, Lancaster University);
- Robson Rhodes;
- Skill: the National Bureau for Students with Disabilities;
- Unison;
- University and College Union; and
- Universities UK.

APPENDIX TWO Supplementary statistics

1. Institutions' performance in comparison with benchmark

28 Rates of continuation compared with benchmark, 2004-05

Institutions with similar student intakes and subject mixes, and therefore similar benchmarks, can have very different rates of continuation.

	Institutions' continuation rate range		
Benchmark	**Lowest**	**Highest**	**Number of institutions**
97.0 – 97.9	98.5	98.6	2
96.0 – 96.9	93.0	97.8	8
95.0 – 95.9	95.0	98.8	5
94.0 – 94.9	93.7	96.6	11
93.0 – 93.9	83.3	96.0	8
92.0 – 92.9	90.0	94.9	6
91.0 – 91.9	89.1	94.6	7
90.0 – 90.9	81.7	95.4	22
89.0 – 89.9	86.2	95.8	23
88.0 – 88.9	85.5	95.3	17
87.0 – 87.9	87.1	89.4	2
86.0 – 86.9	81.6	88.7	5
85.0 – 85.9	85.2	87.0	2
84.0 – 84.9	85.3	85.3	1

National Audit Office analysis of Higher Education Statistics Agency performance indicators

NOTE

The analysis is based on full-time, first-degree students.

29 Institutions' continuation rates and benchmarks 2001-02 to 2004-05

Institution	Continuation rate 2001-02 (%)	Benchmark 2001-02 (%)	Continuation rate 2004-05 (%)	Benchmark 2004-05 (%)	Change in continuation rate (2001-02 to 2004-05) (% points)
Anglia Ruskin University	90.9	87.5	87.1	87.9	–3.8
Arts Institute at Bournemouth	90.9	90.6	93.6	89.8	2.7
University of the Arts London	92.6	90.4	91.1	91.8	–1.5
Aston University	94.7	93.6	93.1	93.0	–1.6
University of Bath	97.7	95.6	96.6	95.7	–1.1
Bath Spa University	90.5	89.4	91.4	90.6	0.9
University of Bedfordshire	88.2	88.0	86.2	86.8	–2.0
University of Birmingham	94.1	94.5	94.0	94.9	–0.1
Bishop Grosseteste University College, Lincoln	93.8	91.5	92.4	92.5	–1.4
University of Bolton	78.2	85.8	81.6	86.3	3.4
Bournemouth University	91.4	90.9	91.0	90.3	–0.4
University of Bradford	89.0	90.1	89.8	89.7	0.8
University of Brighton	90.8	90.5	92.4	90.6	1.6
University of Bristol	97.0	96.6	97.3	96.5	0.3
Brunel University	93.3	90.4	92.7	90.9	–0.6
Buckinghamshire Chilterns University College	89.4	88.2	89.6	88.0	0.2
Canterbury Christ Church University	90.1	89.8	91.0	90.0	0.9
University of Central England in Birmingham	91.2	88.8	90.0	88.9	–1.2
University of Central Lancashire	86.5	88.5	87.9	88.1	1.4
Central School of Speech and Drama	96.0	90.0	94.6	91.4	–1.4
University of Chester	90.1	89.9	81.7	90.1	–8.4
University of Chichester	87.9	89.2	94.4	90.0	6.5
City University, London	91.3	91.4	88.8	89.8	–2.5
Conservatoire for Dance and Drama[1]	87.1	89.7	95.8	89.8	8.7
Coventry University	90.3	89.3	87.3	89.0	–3.0
Cumbria Institute of the Arts	90.0	88.7	90.8	89.9	0.8
Dartington College of Arts	87.7	89.8	90.7	90.3	3.0
De Montfort University	90.4	89.6	90.6	90.0	0.2
University of Derby	87.7	87.8	87.8	86.9	0.1
University of Durham	98.0	95.7	96.9	96.4	–1.1
University of East Anglia	91.0	92.2	96.0	93.6	5.0
University of East London	85.2	86.2	85.2	85.4	0.0
Edge Hill University	86.4	88.8	89.2	89.4	2.8
University of Essex	89.8	90.9	89.1	91.9	–0.7
University of Exeter	97.3	94.4	96.6	94.2	–0.7
University College Falmouth	92.1	90.5	93.5	90.8	1.4
University of Gloucestershire	87.9	89.3	92.6	89.3	4.7
Goldsmiths College, University of London	91.9	90.4	89.3	90.3	–2.6
University of Greenwich	86.4	87.3	89.4	87.6	3.0
University of Hertfordshire	90.3	88.5	91.1	89.3	0.8
Harper Adams University College	83.7	86.6	95.4	90.9	11.7
University of Huddersfield	88.0	88.7	88.5	89.2	0.5
University of Hull	92.1	90.2	92.0	92.7	–0.1
Imperial College London	96.3	97.0	95.4	96.7	–0.9
Keele University	96.9	91.9	94.1	93.1	–2.8

29 Institutions' continuation rates and benchmarks 2001-02 to 2004-05 *continued*

Institution	Continuation rate 2001-02 (%)	Benchmark 2001-02 (%)	Continuation rate 2004-05 (%)	Benchmark 2004-05 (%)	Change in continuation rate (2001-02 to 2004-05) (% points)
University of Kent	92.4	91.3	92.9	91.3	0.5
King's College London	94.4	94.7	95.3	94.7	0.9
Kingston University	90.6	88.9	91.2	89.3	0.6
Lancaster University	95.3	93.9	95.0	94.4	–0.3
University of Leeds	95.1	94.1	93.7	94.7	–1.4
Leeds Metropolitan University	90.9	88.4	91.3	89.1	0.4
University of Leicester	92.6	93.9	93.7	94.2	1.1
University of Lincoln	86.6	88.3	91.0	90.3	4.4
University of Liverpool	92.5	93.1	94.9	94.3	2.4
Liverpool Hope University	85.0	87.9	85.7	88.7	0.7
Liverpool John Moores University	87.8	89.4	87.7	89.6	–0.1
University of London	96.7	91.4	83.3	93.8	–13.4
London Metropolitan University	82.4	85.7	84.5	86.2	2.1
London School of Economics and Political Science	94.8	96.2	94.5	96.5	–0.3
London South Bank University	87.0	85.6	87.0	85.5	0.0
Loughborough University	96.0	94.0	95.6	93.6	–0.4
University of Manchester[1]	94.5	94.2	95.6	94.8	1.1
Manchester Metropolitan University	88.2	88.7	87.6	89.6	–0.6
Middlesex University	84.8	86.8	88.7	86.9	3.9
Newcastle University	94.9	94.2	96.2	95.0	1.3
Newman College of Higher Education	93.9	89.7	90.9	89.3	–3.0
University of Northampton	88.8	89.0	87.0	89.0	–1.8
University of Northumbria at Newcastle	91.6	89.3	89.9	90.2	–1.7
Norwich School of Art and Design	92.1	90.1	93.7	89.2	1.6
University of Nottingham	98.1	96.0	96.8	96.1	–1.3
Nottingham Trent University	93.1	91.1	93.0	91.7	–0.1
University of Oxford	98.7	97.5	98.6	97.3	–0.1
Oxford Brookes University	90.8	90.0	92.1	91.2	1.3
University of Plymouth	92.8	89.7	91.7	88.3	–1.1
University of Portsmouth	90.3	89.6	91.7	89.3	1.4
Queen Mary, University of London	91.3	91.8	92.4	93.1	1.1
Ravensbourne College of Design and Communication	86.0	89.0	92.1	89.6	6.1
University of Reading	93.2	93.3	94.2	94.0	1.0
Roehampton University	84.5	88.8	86.2	89.4	1.7
Rose Bruford College	95.3	91.1	89.5	90.9	–5.8
Royal Academy of Music	88.7	93.6	94.0	93.7	5.3
Royal Agricultural College	94.9	89.8	92.3	91.4	–2.6
Royal College of Music	96.6	89.9	93.6	88.0	–3.0
Royal Holloway, University of London	95.8	94.1	94.3	93.9	–1.5
Royal Northern College of Music	90.0	93.4	95.3	88.2	5.3
Royal Veterinary College	98.7	98.4	98.5	97.0	–0.2
St George's Hospital Medical School	97.5	95.2	98.8	95.0	1.3
College of St Mark and St John	92.0	88.8	89.1	89.0	–2.9
St Martin's College	92.2	90.1	88.8	90.5	–3.4

29 Institutions' continuation rates and benchmarks 2001-02 to 2004-05 *continued*

Institution	Continuation rate 2001-02 (%)	Benchmark 2001-02 (%)	Continuation rate 2004-05 (%)	Benchmark 2004-05 (%)	Change in continuation rate (2001-02 to 2004-05) (% points)
St Mary's University College (Twickenham)	90.8	89.7	94.4	89.8	3.6
University of Salford	89.6	89.5	88.8	89.0	-0.8
School of Oriental and African Studies	84.8	91.2	90.0	92.1	5.2
School of Pharmacy	97.5	94.6	95.6	94.1	-1.9
University of Sheffield	97.0	95.3	96.7	95.3	-0.3
Sheffield Hallam University	91.2	90.1	92.3	90.5	1.1
University of Southampton	94.8	93.7	94.7	94.2	-0.1
Southampton Solent University	88.8	88.7	89.7	88.1	0.9
Staffordshire University	89.0	88.8	88.5	88.8	-0.5
University of Sunderland	85.3	88.8	85.5	88.7	0.2
University of Surrey	93.0	92.2	93.6	92.4	0.6
University of Sussex	90.7	92.6	91.6	92.9	0.9
University of Teesside	89.7	88.3	90.8	88.1	1.1
Thames Valley University	84.3	86.1	85.3	84.5	1.0
Trinity and All Saints	92.4	91.2	90.6	90.4	-1.8
Trinity Laban	88.4	93.0	92.9	88.1	4.5
University College for the Creative Arts[1]	90.4	90.6	90.9	90.7	0.5
University College London	95.4	95.2	95.0	95.1	-0.4
University of Warwick	96.8	96.1	97.8	96.3	1.0
University of the West of England, Bristol	88.9	89.5	90.0	90.5	1.1
University of Westminster	86.9	88.2	88.5	88.8	1.6
Wimbledon College of Art	91.2	91.7	94.9	92.1	3.7
University of Winchester	93.3	90.7	92.6	90.7	-0.7
University of Wolverhampton	85.9	88.0	86.4	88.0	0.5
University of Worcester	85.0	88.5	87.8	88.7	2.8
Writtle College	88.9	85.4	86.4	88.3	-2.5
University of York	95.7	95.8	96.7	96.0	1.0
York St John University	89.8	90.5	90.7	90.9	0.9

Source: National Audit Office analysis of Funding Council and Higher Education Statistics Agency performance indicator data

NOTES

1 For higher education institutions that merged between 2001-02 to 2004-05, we have calculated an average of their 2001-02 continuation rates and 2001-02 benchmarks weighted by their student numbers. These institutions are the Conservatoire for Dance and Drama and Northern School of Contemporary Dance (which become the Conservatoire for Dance and Drama); the Kent Institute of Art and Design and the Surrey Institute of Art and Design (which became the University College for the Creative Arts); University of Manchester and University of Manchester Institute of Science and Technology (which continued as the University of Manchester). No adjustment is made for the small number of institutions that merged with or incorporated colleges of further education.

2 This includes only institutions with data for both years.

2. Trends in student characteristics

30 Personal characteristics of entrants to full-time, first-degree courses 2002-03 to 2005-06

As participation has increased, it has also widened in some respects.

	2002-03 %	2003-04 %	2004-05 %	2005-06 %
Black and minority ethnic	20.3	20.6	21.8	22.2
Has a disability	6.3	6.7	7.3	7.6
Female	53.3	54.0	54.4	54.4
21 or over on entry	22.9	23.0	22.4	21.4
'Working class'[1]	29.5	29.8	29.4	30.7
Low participation neighbourhoods	27.4	28.2	28.1	28.9

Source: National Audit Office analysis of Higher Education Statistics Agency individual student data

NOTES

1 Socio-economic groups 4-7: Small employers and own account workers, Lower supervisory and technical occupations, Semi-routine occupations, Routine occupations.

2 United Kingdom domiciled first-degree students in English higher education institutions.

31 Entry qualifications of entrants to full-time, first-degree courses 2002-03 to 2005-06

A level and equivalent qualifications remain the most common entry qualifications for entrants to higher education.

	2002-03 %	2003-04 %	2004-05 %	2005-06 %
A levels and equivalents[1]	78.0	78.3	80.5	81.2
Higher education	9.3	9.5	8.8	8.7
Foundation/ access courses	5.9	5.8	5.8	5.9
No academic or vocational qualifications	1.5	1.5	1.3	1.2
Unknown/other	5.3	4.9	3.6	3.0
Total	100.0	100.0	100.0	100.0

Source: National Audit Office analysis of Higher Education Statistics Agency individual student data

NOTES

1 Equivalents include, for example, BTEC National Diplomas and Baccalaureates.

2 United Kingdom domiciled first-degree students in English higher education institutions.

32 Study characteristics of entrants to undergraduate courses 2002-03 to 2005-06

There have been some small changes in how students engage with higher education.

	2002-03 %	2003-04 %	2004-05 %	2005-06 %
Mode of study				
Part-time	44.7	45.4	44.5	44.9
Qualification sought				
First degree	52.6	56.5	56.9	57.9
Higher National Diplomas and Certificates	4.1	3.2	2.8	2.2
Foundation degrees	1.4	2.3	2.8	3.5
Other undergraduate courses	41.9	38.0	37.5	36.4
Total	100.0	100.0	100.0	100.0

Source: National Audit Office analysis of Higher Education Statistics Agency individual student data

NOTE

1 United Kingdom domiciled undergraduates in English higher education institutions.

3. Trends in subject choice and subject continuation rates

33 Applicants accepting places on undergraduate courses 2002-03 and 2006-07

The number of applicants accepting places increased over the last five years, and there have been changes in the mix of subjects.

Subject	2002-03	2006-07	Percentage increase/ decrease 2002 to 2006
Architecture, Building and Planning	5,370	7,409	38
Subjects allied to Medicine	18,598	24,485	32
Education	10,413	12,969	25
Social Studies	21,974	25,909	18
Technologies	1,938	2,246	16
Medicine and Dentistry	7,159	8,239	15
Creative Arts and Design	34,924	39,908	14
Law	14,405	16,026	11
Biological Sciences	26,984	29,051	8
Veterinary Science, Agriculture and related	3,703	3,982	8
Linguistics, Classics and related	10,171	10,737	6
Mass Communications and Documentation	8,060	8,463	5
Physical Sciences	13,593	13,928	2
History and Philosophical studies	12,256	12,437	1
European Languages, Literature and related	3,695	3,646	–1
Business and Administration studies	38,428	37,373	–3
Combined subjects	53,120	51,310	–3
Engineering	16,840	14,814	–12
Non-European Languages and related	2,076	1,586	–24
Mathematical and Computer Science	28,018	21,046	–25
All subjects	**331,725**	**345,564**	**4**

Source: National Audit Office analysis of UCAS applications and acceptances data

NOTE

Based on all United Kingdom domiciled students accepting places on full-time courses at United Kingdom institutions through UCAS. This includes degrees and other undergraduate courses.

34 Continuation by subject over time 2002-03 to 2004-05

There are wide variations in the continuation rates of different subjects.

Subject	Full-time undergraduates 2002-03 (%)	Full-time undergraduates 2003-04 (%)	Full-time undergraduates 2004-05 (%)	Part-time undergraduates 2002-03 (%)	Part-time undergraduates 2003-04 (%)	Part-time undergraduates 2004-05 (%)
Medicine and Dentistry	97.3	97.5	97.9	–	–	–
Subjects allied to Medicine	89.3	90.7	90.2	61.0	60.8	63.8
Biological Sciences	89.6	90.5	91.7	57.4	76.8	74.9
Veterinary Sciences, Agriculture and related subjects	88.9	89.6	89.4	65.3	59.4	51.3
Physical Sciences	91.4	93.0	93.0	57.4	67.6	70.0
Mathematical and Computer Sciences	85.7	88.0	88.1	58.7	65.7	64.6
Engineering	86.3	87.9	88.3	70.0	68.4	67.5
Technologies	85.4	89.9	91.3	70.2	74.5	39.3
Architecture, Building and Planning	85.9	87.9	89.3	69.0	75.7	75.8
Social studies	90.3	91.5	91.3	59.8	75.4	71.5
Law	90.3	91.7	92.2	54.6	72.7	69.7
Business and Administrative studies	86.9	88.1	88.9	56.6	62.4	63.9
Mass Communications and Documentation	88.9	90.2	89.4	38.7	40.0	55.4
Linguistics, Classics and related subjects	91.7	91.8	92.9	46.0	66.0	63.2
European Languages, Literature and related subjects	90.5	92.3	93.2	36.0	44.6	53.0
Eastern, Asiatic, African, American and Australasian Languages, Literature and related subjects	88.5	90.9	92.2	36.8	47.0	43.3
Historical and Philosophical studies	91.5	92.1	93.7	52.2	57.2	57.3
Creative Arts and Design	89.5	89.6	89.8	50.1	50.3	52.1
Education	89.5	90.1	90.8	63.4	71.6	69.0
Combined subjects	81.0	84.2	82.9	68.3	57.8	51.6

Source: National Audit Office analysis of Higher Education Statistics Agency individual student data

APPENDIX THREE

Common reasons for withdrawal

35 Common reasons for students' withdrawal from courses

Students withdraw from courses for a variety of inter-related reasons.

Personal reasons

- Student may fall mentally or physically ill, or a longstanding problem may worsen
- Homesickness is thought to be a common cause of very early withdrawal, especially among young women and students from rural areas
- Balancing domestic obligations against study requirements – for example, childcare or elder care arrangements may collapse

Lack of integration

- An absence of positive ties means students fail to 'bond' with the institution and are more easily deterred when another issue arises
- Students 'drift away' without institutions knowing why or when they have withdrawn
- Difficulty in fitting in socially — students from deprived areas may feel culturally isolated

Dissatisfaction with course/institution

- The student may feel bored or otherwise dissatisfied with the standard of tuition
- The course may not lead to the professional accreditation they were seeking

Lack of preparedness

- The course content may not be what the student was expecting
- Students may not have the study skills in place for success or realise the extent to which progress will rely on self-direction
- Students may not realise the level of commitment required to succeed
- The level of the course may be too difficult
- Late applications for Disabled Students' Allowances may mean the student does not have the support and equipment in place at the start of term

Wrong choice of course

- Students may not have researched their choice deeply, especially if entering late
- Students may be channelled into inappropriate subjects (especially working class men)
- Lack of information about higher education can lead to stereotypical choices of course and institution (especially students from disadvantaged areas)
- Working class students may lack the confidence to change course or institution

Financial reasons

- Students no longer pay tuition fees up-front, but they may still incur debt
- The student may struggle to balance working while studying. Working in excess of 15 hours a week has been found to reduce chances of progression
- Benefits and allowances may not come through in time to meet financial commitments
- Fear of debt, more than actual levels of debt, may be an issue for some students
- Limited funds may mean students from disadvantaged backgrounds cut short their studies
- Students may have unrealistic lifestyle expectations which drives them into debt and early leaving (especially young men)

To take up a more attractive opportunity

- Attending the university or college may allow a student to achieve their career goals without necessarily completing the course
- Taking time out to travel
- Late realisation of academic interests or career goals

Sources: Caldwell-Brodie, J et al (2007), *Exhausting avenues? The impact of term-time employment on progression and retention*, conference paper, September 2006. Cook A (2004) *Heading them off at the pass: predicting retention problems*, Higher Education Academy; Davies R and Elias P (2003) *Dropping out: A study of early leavers from higher education*; Forsyth A and Furlong A (2003) *Losing out? Socioeconomic disadvantage and experience in further and higher education*, Joseph Rowntree Foundation; Harrison N (2006) *Journal of Further and Higher Education*, 'The impact of negative experiences, dissatisfaction and attachment on first year undergraduate withdrawal' Vol. 30, No. 4, pp. 377–391; Heist (2007) *Early Leavers Research: Report prepared for Edge Hill University*; National Audit Office (2002) *Improving student achievement in English higher education*, HC 486; Quinn J et al (2005) *From life crisis to lifelong learning: Rethinking working-class 'drop out' from higher education*, Joseph Rowntree Foundation.

APPENDIX FOUR

Statistical notes

1. Predicting higher education institutions' continuation rates (paragraph 1.20)

We used the 'linear regression' technique to assess which factors were linked with institutions' continuation rates. Our model was based on data supplied by 121 institutions for the Higher Education Statistics Agency's 'Individual Student Record' for entrants in the 2004-05 academic year. The regression model predicts the relationship between an institution's continuation rate and a number of variables, such as the proportions of students from particular social groups or the average A level tariff score of students at the institution.

We used 'stepwise' linear regression to predict how the continuation rate changes as a range of variables change – stepwise linear regression adds variables one at a time, and then includes the most significant variable. It then repeats the exercise by adding the remaining variables one at time and adding the most significant and then excluding any variables which are no longer significant after the new variable has been included. This iterative process continues until no further variables can be added or excluded from the model.

The 'R-square' statistic indicates that our model explains 71 per cent of the variation in continuation rates of full-time students: a reasonably good model. We also constructed a model for part-time students, but the R-square statistic was only 21 per cent: this is not a good model and so has not been used in the report.

Results

The calculations identified eight variables that had a significant relationship with continuation:

Variable	Coefficient	Significance
Proportion of students studying Medicine and Dentistry	0.134	0.0001
Proportion of students studying Education	0.131	0.0000
Proportion of students studying Subjects allied to Medicine	0.035	0.0389
Proportion of students studying Creative Arts and Design	0.033	0.0003
Average participation neighbourhood	0.029	0.0001
Average tariff score	0.006	0.0000
Proportion of students studying European Languages, Literature and related subjects	–0.060	0.0068
Proportion of students aged 21 or more	–0.070	0.0021
(Constant	0.785	0.0000)

For the six variables with a positive coefficient, an increase in the value of the variable is associated with an **increase** in continuation.

For the two variables with a negative coefficient, an increase in the value of the variable is a **reduction** in continuation.

A number of other variables relating to an institution's student intake were tested but found not to be statistically significant in explaining variations between institutions. The variables fell within the following headings:

- ethnicity;
- gender;
- socio-economic classifications;
- students with a foundation degree;
- status regarding Disabled Students' Allowances; and
- course subject categories.

2. Calculating students' chances of continuing to a second year (Figure 16)

To better understand the factors influencing the chances of continuation for students, we constructed two further models, one for full-time and another for part-time students. Again, we used the data from the Higher Education Statistics Agency's 'Individual Student Record' (299,000 full-time students and 229,000 part-time students) for entrants in the 2004-05 academic year. We used 'logistic regression' because the outcome for students can only be 'continue' or 'not continue'.

The regression model measures the relationship between student continuation and a number of variables, such as the age of a student and the subject studied. The model takes account of the different relationships between continuation and the variables in the model at the same time. We included some variables in the model even though they were not significant, because we still wanted to take account of the effect of those variables.

The results are presented in the table below in the form of odds ratios. Odds ratios compare the probabilities of continuation for two groups of students whilst other characteristics remain constant. An odds ratio of 1.00 indicates that continuation is equally likely in both groups of student. An odds ratio greater than 1.00 indicates that continuation is more likely in the first group. For example, the chances of a full-time, female student continuing are 91.6 to 8.4; those of a male student 89.4 to 10.6. The odds ratio is therefore: 91.6 ÷ 8.4 = 10.9 (students that continue for every one that leaves early) divided by 89.4 ÷ 10.6 = 8.4, which equals 1.3.

Results

The calculations produced the following results.

Factor	Full time		Part time		Comparator group
	Odds ratio	Significance	Odds ratio	Significance	
Age	0.90	0.000	1.00	0.000	(Not applicable)
21 and over	0.10	0.000			Under 21
21 and over multiplied by age (interaction variable)	1.12	0.000			(Not applicable)
Male	0.77	0.000	0.90	0.000	Female
Other white background	1.23	0.000	1.04	0.066	White
Black	1.06	0.015	0.97	0.064	"
Pakistani and Bangladeshi	1.09	0.002	0.81	0.000	"
Indian and Chinese	1.20	0.000	0.90	0.000	"
Other Asian background	1.18	0.002	0.83	0.000	"
Mixed race	1.00	0.479	0.97	0.261	"
Other Ethnic background	0.97	0.327	0.86	0.001	"
Ethnicity not known	0.68	0.000	0.84	0.000	"
Has a declared disability	1.05	0.033	1.11	0.000	No declared disability
Disability status unknown	1.12	0.140	1.08	0.003	"
Lowest participation neighbourhood	0.84	0.000	0.93	0.000	Highest participation neighbourhood
2nd lowest participation neighbourhood	0.93	0.000	0.96	0.001	
Middle participation neighbourhood	0.94	0.002	0.99	0.218	"
2nd highest participation neighbourhood	1.02	0.218	0.97	0.023	"
Participation neighbourhood unknown	0.82	0.000	0.95	0.067	"
Socio-economic classification 4-7	0.91	0.000	1.30	0.001	Socio-economic classification 1-3
Socio-economic classification unknown	0.78	0.000	0.87	0.001	

Factor	Full time		Part time		Comparator group
	Odds ratio	Significance	Odds ratio	Significance	
Studying a strategically important science, technology, engineering or mathematical subject	0.84	0.000	0.84	0.000	Studying a different subject
Studying a modern foreign language	0.70	0.000	1.21	0.159	"
On a foundation degree in the previous year	1.32	0.001	1.91	0.000	Not on foundation degree in the previous year
Tariff score	1.12	0.000	1.06	0.000	(Not applicable)
No tariff score available	1.05	0.031	0.87	0.000	Tariff score available
Attending a faith-based institution	0.87	0.044	1.28	0.155	Attending a different type of institution
Attending a Russell Group institution	1.24	0.002	1.05	0.420	"
Attending a 94 Group institution[1]	1.06	0.210	0.75	0.094	"
Attending a Campaigning for Modern Universities institution[2]	0.89	0.027	1.08	0.343	"
Attending a GuildHE institution	1.09	0.124	1.09	0.350	"
Student studying under a franchise agreement	0.70	0.000	1.56	0.000	Student not studying under franchise agreement
Student studying under a mixed franchise agreement	0.84	0.019	1.65	0.000	"
Studying other undergraduate courses	0.92	0.000			Studying first degree
Study aim is a foundation degree			1.29	0.000	"
Study aim is a Higher National Diploma/Certificate			1.16	0.159	"
Study aim is credits			0.29	0.000	"
Study aim is other undergraduate qualifications			0.89	0.000	"
Constant	69.08	0.000	2.53	0.000	(Not applicable)

NOTES

1 Group of 19 research-intensive institutions.

2 Group of universities forming in 1992.

3 Significance figures greater than 0.050 indicate that the result is not statistically significant.

3. A note on statistical tests used

Levene's Equality of Variance test

The Levene statistic tests whether the variations of two or more groups are equal. In this case the two groups are institutions' continuation rates for 2001-02 and 2004-05.

Significance levels

A significance level for model coefficients gives the probability that the coefficient is actually zero. The smaller the significance level the stronger the evidence that the coefficient is different from zero, and hence the stronger the relationship between the continuation rate and that particular factor.

A five per cent significance level indicates that there is only a one in twenty probability that the result we see is due to chance. Throughout this report we have used the five per cent significance level when we refer to a result as statistically significant. In the statistical tables, significant results are those for which the significance level is 0.05 or lower.

4. Classification of institutions, 2004-05, as used in Figure 13

Pre-1992 universities (excluding The Russell Group)

Aston University
Brunel University
City University, London
Goldsmiths College, University of London
Keele University
Lancaster University
Loughborough University
Queen Mary, University of London
Royal Holloway, University of London
University of Bath
University of Bradford
University of Durham
University of East Anglia
University of Essex
University of Exeter
University of Hull
University of Kent
University of Leicester
University of London
University of Reading
University of Salford
University of Surrey
University of Sussex
University of York

The Russell Group

Imperial College London
King's College London
London School of Economics and Political Science
Newcastle University
University College London
University of Birmingham
University of Bristol
University of Leeds
University of Liverpool
University of Manchester
University of Nottingham
University of Oxford
University of Sheffield
University of Southampton
University of Warwick

Post-1992 universities

Anglia Ruskin University
Bath Spa University
Bournemouth University
Coventry University
De Montfort University
Edge Hill University
Kingston University
Leeds Metropolitan University
Liverpool Hope University
Liverpool John Moores University
London Metropolitan University
London South Bank University
Manchester Metropolitan University
Middlesex University
Nottingham Trent University
Oxford Brookes University
Sheffield Hallam University
Southampton Solent University
Staffordshire University
Thames Valley University
University of Bedfordshire
University of Bolton
University of Brighton
University of Central England in Birmingham
University of Central Lancashire
University of Chester
University of Chichester
University of Derby
University of East London
University of Gloucestershire
University of Greenwich
University of Hertfordshire
University of Huddersfield
University of Lincoln
University of Northampton
University of Northumbria at Newcastle
University of Plymouth
University of Portsmouth
University of Sunderland
University of Teesside
University of the West of England, Bristol
University of Westminster
University of Winchester
University of Wolverhampton
University of Worcester

Small and specialist institutions

Bishop Grosseteste University College, Lincoln
Canterbury Christ Church University
College of St Mark and St John
Newman College of Higher Education
Roehampton University
St Martin's College
St Mary's University College (Twickenham)
Trinity and All Saints
York St John University
Royal Academy of Music
Royal College of Music
Royal Northern College of Music
Trinity Laban
Arts Institute at Bournemouth
Central School of Speech and Drama
Conservatoire for Dance and Drama
Courtauld Institute of Art
Cumbria Institute of the Arts
Dartington College of Arts
Norwich School of Art and Design
Ravensbourne College of Design and Communication
Rose Bruford College
University College Falmouth
University College for the Creative Arts
University of the Arts London
Wimbledon College of Art
Royal Agricultural College
Royal Veterinary College
School of Oriental and African Studies
School of Pharmacy
St George's Hospital Medical School
Birmingham College of Food, Tourism and Creative Studies
Buckinghamshire Chilterns University College
Harper Adams University College
Writtle College

APPENDIX FIVE

Recommendations from the 58th Report from the Committee of Public Accounts, 2001-02

The Committee of Public Accounts drew eight conclusions from its report on *Improving student achievement in English higher education*, five of which are relevant to student retention. In response the then Department for Education and Skills and the Funding Council committed to a number of actions. These are detailed below, along with an assessment by the National Audit Office of the progress that has been made.

Committee of Public Accounts' recommendation	**Department's and Funding Council's response to recommendations in the Treasury Minute**	**Progress to date**
The Funding Council pays higher education institutions a premium, based on student home postcodes, as a broad proxy for the extra costs institutions incur on students from poorer backgrounds, for example on focused recruitment and extra teaching support. The Funding Council recognises that the 'postcode' system is not ideal, especially for students from rural areas or inner cities. In its review of the additional costs higher education institutions bear and of the methodology used to allocate widening participation funding, it should look for ways of better targeting the £31 million involved.	The Department and the Funding Council agreed that they needed better ways of targeting the widening participation allocation. The Funding Council consulted the sector over summer 2002 on the way in which the funding is allocated, and, at the time of the Treasury Minute, was considering the appropriate level of funding and how it might be distributed to match need more closely.	A 2003 review commissioned by the Funding Council estimated that the additional cost per widening participation student was around £900 on average (paragraph 2.9). From 2003-04, the Funding Council substantially increased the widening participation funding by introducing the improving retention element, financed by an overall reduction in the rest of the teaching grant (paragraph 2.10.) From 2004-05, the Funding Council revised the funding method for the widening access element. It is now based on higher education participation rates by ward (for young, full-time undergraduates) and average educational achievement by ward (for part-time and mature, full-time undergraduates) (paragraph 2.10).
One reason why students leave higher education without completing their qualification, or fail, is that they are not well prepared in key skills before they start. **Higher education institutions** therefore have to identify knowledge and skills gaps and provide support to students, for example remedial or catch-up courses in mathematics in the first year. **The Department** needs to ensure that the difficulties being experienced by institutions are fed into curriculum development and back to schools, through the work of the Qualifications and Curriculum Authority.	The Department pledged to work with the sector to pilot and evaluate different approaches to bridging the gap between students' prior knowledge and the requirements of higher education study. The Department indicated that the Government would keep under review students' progress between A level and degree courses. *(From the Government's response to the Roberts Review in July 2002).* The Department was working with the Qualifications and Curriculum Authority to raise the profile and take up of key-skills units with the intention of saving institutions from having to provide remedial provision.	Institutions continue to address deficits in students' study skills (paragraphs 3.14 to 3.16).

Committee of Public Accounts' recommendation ***continued***	**Department's and Funding Council's response to recommendations in the Treasury Minute** ***continued***	**Progress to date** ***continued***
Overall achievement in higher education compares favourably with other industrialised nations. Significant improvement depends on raising students' academic performance in schools, which will take time. Meanwhile, **the Funding Council** should continue to bear down on very wide variations in performance between institutions, for example success rates ranging from 48 per cent to 98 per cent. It should develop an action plan focusing on under-performing institutions, in consultation with **the Department.**	The Funding Council had already developed an action plan focused on retention, and spent approximately £3 million across three years (2003-05) on the national co-ordination team for widening participation: Action on Access. Action on Access supports the sector in working on retention and widening participation.	The Funding Council redistributed part of the teaching grant to institutions on the basis of their students' characteristics and qualifications, to enable them to better support students more likely not to continue their studies (paragraph 2.10). Institutional performance was in a slightly narrower range in 2004-05 compared with 2001-02, but with a similar distribution (paragraph 11). More institutions (42) have seen an increase in their continuation rate by one percentage point or more than have seen a similar decrease (30 institutions) (paragraph 11). Our analysis did not find conclusive evidence regarding the impact on institutions' continuation rates of this change in funding, owing to there being only a small number of years of data available (paragraph 14).
Potential students rely on good information to ensure they get on the course they want and that it meets their expectations. The quality of information is improving, for example through on-line services such as the Higher Education Research Database. In their information to potential students, **institutions** should draw on the research conducted by the National Audit Office to provide information on areas such as course content, methods of assessment, the amount of time students should spend at their studies, any ancillary costs, and success rates of past students.	From 2002-03 onwards "institutions are expected to make publicly available a range of up-to-date information on quality and standards. It is intended to make this information accessible on the internet in a user-friendly format in a way which will help applicants make informed choices." The Government was also "developing an electronic portal... to provide a 'one stop shop' on all higher education matters".	The National Student Survey now provides information on the quality of the student experience to new applicants. The Teaching Quality Information website was set up to make this information available to potential students. However, this website has been under-used, and following a review it will be revised and relaunched (paragraphs 2.17 and 2.18). An additional website, the 'Aimhigher' site has been established to provide information on higher education to students from under-represented groups (paragraph 2.17).
The Department should review the support available for disabled students, including allowances from local authorities, so as to give these students greater certainty over support before they have to decide on whether to accept a place in higher education, to remove any disincentives to participation.	The Department agreed that it was important that disabled students are properly supported and know the level of support they can expect to receive before they decide whether to enter higher education. A 2001 review of the administration of the Disabled Students' Allowances, undertaken by Skill (the National Bureau for Students with Disabilities), made recommendations to improve access to the scheme. The Department was implementing the recommendations in consultation with Skill and other partners.	In 2004, the Department set up the Disabled Students Allowance Quality Assurance Group to provide an integrated quality assurance service to people accessing the scheme. The Group comprised representatives from local authorities, assessment centres, equipment suppliers, higher education institutions, Skill (as observers) and the National Union of Students.

GLOSSARY

Benchmarks (for continuation)	Because there are such differences between institutions, the average values for the whole of the higher education sector are not necessarily helpful when comparing higher education institutions. The Higher Education Statistics Agency therefore calculates a sector average which is then adjusted for each institution to take into account some of the factors which contribute to the differences between them. The factors allowed for are subject of study, qualifications on entry and age on entry (young or mature). The average, adjusted for these factors, is called the adjusted sector benchmark. The benchmarks are calculated using data from all United Kingdom institutions.
Completion	For the purposes of the performance indicators published by the Higher Education Statistics Agency, completion refers to the proportion of new students projected to obtain a degree at their original institution within 15 years. For the Funding Council's funding purposes, completion means completing the year of study: that is, undergoing the final assessment of, or otherwise passing, each module attempted in the year. For its recurrent funding allocations to institutions, the Funding Council does not count students that do not complete their year of study.
Continuation	The proportion of the annual intake of new students who return to higher education in the subsequent year.
Credit	An indicator of the amount and level of learning that is expected or has been achieved.
Credit value	The number of credits a student may achieve through successful completion of a unit or programme of study.
Foundation degree	Starting in September 2001, foundation degrees are employment-related, higher education qualifications at Level 5 in the National Qualifications Framework, just below honours degree level. They are typically two years long when studied full-time and are offered by both higher and further education institutions.
Full-time student	Students are recorded as studying full-time if they are charged a full-time fee and are normally required to attend the institution, or elsewhere (for example if on sandwich courses), for periods amounting to at least 24 weeks within the year of study; and during that time they are normally expected to undertake periods of study, tuition or work experience which amount to an average of at least 21 hours per week.

Higher Education students	Those students on programmes of study for which the level of instruction is above that of Level 3 of the National Qualifications Framework (such as A levels).
Low participation neighbourhoods	Geodemographic areas for which the participation rate is less than two-thirds of the United Kingdom average rate.
Mature student	Those students who are aged 21 or over at 30 September of the academic year in which they enter higher education.
Non traditional student	The definition varies, but can include undergraduates: ■ from low participation neighbourhoods (on basis of postcodes); ■ with a disability; ■ who are mature; ■ studying part time; ■ from households with a low income; ■ from socio-economic classifications 4-7 ('working class'); ■ from an ethnic minority; and ■ who are the first in their family to enter higher education.
Part-time student	Students are recorded as studying part time if they do not meet the definition of full-time study.
Progression	Act of moving to the next level of a programme of study at end of an academic session. For part-time students it may be successful completion of a specified number of modules.
Survival	An estimate based on the number of new graduates divided by the number of new entrants admitted in a previous year, with a time lag equivalent to the typical length of a full-time degree (Organisation for Economic Co-operation and Development definition).
Undergraduate	Student working towards a first degree, foundation degree, higher education certificate or diploma or equivalent.
Unit/Module	A block of learning with a coherent set of formally identified learning outcomes at a single level.
Young students	Those students who are aged under 21 at 30 September of the academic year in which they enter the institution.

Printed in the UK for the Stationery Office Limited
on behalf of the Controller of Her Majesty's Stationery Office
5560126 07/07 7333